Race and Nationality in American Life

Oscar Handlin was born in New York in 1915 and was educated at Brooklyn College and received the M.A. and Ph.D. degrees from Harvard University. He has subsequently been on the faculty of both of these institutions and is today professor of history at Harvard. He has been awarded the history prize by the Union League Club. In 1941 he was awarded the American History Association J. H. Dumning prize for his book, *Boston Immigrants, 1790–1865*, and in 1952 the Pulitzer Prize for History for *The Uprooted*. Other published works include *Commonwealth: A Study of the Role of Government in the American Economy*, *Adventure in Freedom*, *Chance or Destiny: Turning Points in American History*, and the *Harvard Guide to American History*, of which Professor Handlin is the editor. RACE AND NATIONALITY IN AMERICAN LIFE was first published in 1957.

Race and Nationality in American Life

OSCAR HANDLIN

Doubleday Anchor Books
Doubleday & Company, Inc.
Garden City, New York

COVER BY JEROME GOULD
TYPOGRAPHY BY EDWARD GOREY

Reprinted by arrangement with Little, Brown & Company, Inc., Boston, Mass. Clothbound copies of this work are available from Little, Brown & Company, Inc.

To Charles W. and Mildred Morton

CONTENTS

Introduction

IN THE brief span of the past quarter century we have seen a tragic succession of horrors challenge the assumption, upon which modern civilization rests, that personal dignity is inherent in the condition of human beings.

A blind fury that welled up into indiscriminate destruction animated the Turks in Smyrna in 1922. Ten years thereafter in the Ukraine the rulers of the Soviet Union undertook a systematic extermination of millions in the interests of high policy. And in little more than a decade later the Nazis had set their extermination camps in operation.

These tragic holocausts were all shocking in their indecency. But the cremation ovens evoked a peculiar horror. They revealed that the men who built them were moved by ideas and preconceptions and emotions that negated the oneness of humankind and affirmed the ineradicable differences among peoples. The frightful implications of the racism there expressed are an unforgettable part of Western history. They also have a continuing significance in our own times.

We have learned much about the role of race hatred in these brutal assaults upon our common heritage, and we have accumulated much information concerning the nature and effect of the various divisive doctrines that have attempted to create different categories of men. Serious students have approached the subject by three different avenues. Some have treated racism as a system of ideas, and have tried to discover the origin and to trace the formal development of such ideas in diverse times and places. Other scholars have taken as their point of departure an analysis of the types of personality susceptible to racist influences. There have been very useful examinations of the character structure of individuals, of the channels through which racist conceptions are acquired, and of the agencies through which prejudice is generated and spread. Still a third group of investigators concentrates upon the nature of the background against which prejudice develops, and seeks the causes of prejudice in the structure of society. Each approach can contribute to the understanding, for racism is a complex reaction, the strength of which lies in its many-stranded nature.

The origins of racism lie in the comparatively recent past and we may, in our lifetime, see it run its full course. It is thus susceptible to historical investigation, and an account of the forces that brought it into being may contribute to the comprehension of its nature.

A substantial part of the contents of this volume appeared first in the form of articles, called forth by immediate events. But they have nevertheless a unity of point of view, for they were all composed by a historian who searched the record of the past for clues to the problems of the present. All have been considerably revised and new sections have been written to form an orderly analysis.

The book deals with a general problem, but its point of departure is specific—the condition of the Negro, who, in American society, has been the most notable victim of racism. His degradation was clearly connected with his exploitation, although his exploitation did not altogether explain his degradation. The history of his settlement in America and of the popular conceptions of his character may throw light on the judgments made of his race.

But the idea of race rested on a body of knowledge not limited by national lines and influencing other groups as well as the Negro. Furthermore, it was an idea charged with emotion, and a full understanding of it demands an assessment of the intellectual and emotional context within which it took hold. Dealing with three levels of behavior—rational justification, scientific theory, and emotional reaction—the successive chapters of this work seek insight into one of the portentous human developments of our times.

It may be that the emotions which found one form of expression in race hatred are susceptible, under other conditions, of finding more positive and more creative forms. The indications in our past of the means of channeling these sentiments in constructive directions may have critical implications for the problems of the future.

Race and Exploitation

CHAPTER I

The Origins of Negro Slavery

In the bitter years before the American Civil War, and after, men often turned to history for an explanation of the disastrous difference that divided the nation against itself. It seemed as if some fundamental fault must account for the tragedy that was impending or that had been realized, and it was tempting then to ascribe the troubles of the times to an original separateness between the sections that fought each other in 1861.

The last quarter century has banished from serious historical thinking the ancestral cavaliers and roundheads with whom the rebels and Yankees had peopled their past. But there is still an inclination to accept as present from the start a marked divergence in the character of the labor force—free whites in the North, Negro slaves in the South. Most commonly the sources of that divergence are discovered in geography. In the temperate North, it is held, English ways were transposed intact. But the soil and climate of the South favored the production of staples, most efficiently raised under a regime of plantation slavery. Implicit is the assumption that the Negroes were, from the start, set off by their slavery, and that all the tragic consequences for the South flowed from some original difference in the land and in the people.

However, it is hardly proper to load nature with responsibility for human institutions. Tropical crops and climate persisted in the South after 1865, when its labor system changed, and they were there before it appeared. Negro slavery was not spontaneously produced by heat, humidity, and tobacco. An examination of the condition and status of seventeenth-century labor will show that slavery was not there from the start, that it was not simply imitated from elsewhere, and that it was not a response to any unique qualities in the Negro himself. It emerged rather from the adjustment to American conditions of traditional European institutions.

By the latter half of the eighteenth century slavery was a clearly defined status. It was, the lawbooks explained:

that condition of a natural person, in which, by the operation of law, the application of his physical and mental powers depends . . . upon the will of another . . . and in which he is incapable . . . of . . . holding property [or any other rights] . . . except as the agent or instrument of another. In slavery . . . the state, in ignoring the personality of the slave . . . commits the control of his conduct . . . to the master, together with the power of transferring his authority to another.

Thinking of slavery in that sense, the Englishmen of 1772 could boast with Lord Mansfield that their country had never tolerated the institution; simply to touch the soil of England made men free. But the distinction between slave and free that had become important in the eighteenth century was not a significant distinction at the opening of the seventeenth century. In the earlier period the antithesis of "free" was not "slave" but "unfree"; and, within the condition of unfreedom, law and practice recognized several gradations.

The status that involved the most complete lack of freedom was villenage, a servile condition transmitted from father to son. The villein was limited in the right to hold property or make contracts; he could be bought and sold with the land he worked or without, and had "to do all that the Lord will him command"; while the lord could "rob, beat, and chastise his Villain at his will." It was true that the condition had almost ceased to exist in England itself. But it persisted in Scotland well into the eighteenth century. In law the conception remained important enough to induce Coke, in 1658–1659, to give it a lengthy section in his *Institutes of the Laws of England;* and the analogy with villenage served frequently to define the terms of other forms of servitude.

For law and practice in the seventeenth century comprehended other forms of involuntary bondage. The essential attributes of villenage were fastened on many men not through heredity and ancient custom, as in the case of the villein, but through poverty, crime, or mischance. A debtor, in cases "where there is not sufficient distresse of goods," could be "sold at an outcry." Conviction for vagrancy and vagabondage, even the mere absence of a fixed occupation, exposed the free-born Englishman, at home or in the colonies, to the danger that he might be bound over to the highest bidder, his labor sold for a term. Miscreants who could not pay their fines for a wide range of offenses were punished by servitude on "publick works" or on the estates of individuals under conditions not far different from those of villenage. Such sentences, in the case of the graver felonies, sometimes were for life.

The sale by the head of a household of members of his family entailed a similar kind of involuntary servitude. A husband could thus dispose of his wife, and a father of his children. Indeed, reluctance to part with idle youngsters could bring on the intercession of the public authorities. So, in 1646, Virginia county commissioners were authorized to send to work in the public flaxhouse two youngsters from each county, kept at home by the "fond indulgence or perverse obstinacy" of their parents. Orphans, bastards, and the offspring of servants were similarly subject to disposal at the will of officials.

Moreover, servitude as an estate was not confined to those who fell into it against their wills. It also held many men who entered it by agreement of formal indenture, most commonly for a fixed span of years under conditions contracted for in advance, but occasionally for life, and frequently without definite statement of terms, under the assumption that the custom of the country was definite enough. The poor who wished to come to America could thus barter their labor for the passage.

Early modification in the laws regulating servitude did not, in England or the colonies, alter essentially the nature of the condition. Whether voluntary or involuntary, the status did not involve substantially more freedom in law than villenage. It was not heritable; but servants could be bartered for a profit, sold to the highest bidder for the unpaid debts of their masters, and otherwise transferred like movable goods or chattels. Their capacity to hold property was narrowly limited, as was their right to make contracts. Furthermore, the master had extensive powers of discipline, enforced by physical chastisement or by extension of the term of service. Offenses against the state also brought on punishments different from those meted out to free men; with no property to be fined, the servants were whipped. In every civic, social, and legal attribute these victims of the turbulent displacements of the sixteenth and seventeenth centuries were set apart. Despised by every other order, without apparent means of rising to a more favored place, these men, and their children, and their children's children, seemed mired in a hard, degraded life. That they formed a numerous element in society was nothing to lighten their lot.

The condition of the first Negroes in the continental English colonies must be viewed within the perspective of these conceptions and realities of servitude. As Europeans penetrated the dark continent in search of gold and ivory, they developed incidentally the international trade in blacks. The Dutch in particular found this an attractive means of breaking into the business of the Spanish colonies in America. The government in Madrid persistently refused to permit its dependencies to replenish their labor supply by dealing directly with Africa—a golden opportunity for outsiders able to act as intermediaries. In the course of this exchange through the West Indies, especially through Curaçao, occasional small lots were left along the coast between Virginia and Massachusetts.

Through the first three quarters of the seventeenth century the Negroes, even in the South, were not numerous;

nor were they particularly concentrated in any district. They came into a society in which a large part of the population was to some degree unfree; indeed, in Virginia, for the first two decades of settlement under the company, almost everyone, even tenants and laborers, bore some sort of servile obligation. The Negroes' lack of freedom was not unusual. These newcomers, like so many others, were accepted, bought, and held as servants. They were certainly not well off. But their ill fortune was of a sort they shared with men from England, Scotland, and Ireland, and with the unlucky aborigines held in captivity. Like the others, some Negroes became free, that is, terminated their period of service. Some became artisans, a few became landowners and the masters of other men. The status of Negroes was that of servants, and so they were identified and treated down to the 1660's.

The word "slave" was, of course, used occasionally. It had no meaning in English law, but there was a significant colloquial usage. This was a general term of derogation. It served to express contempt. "O what a rogue and peasant slave am I!" says Hamlet (Act II, Scene 2). It also described the lowborn as contrasted with the gentry. Of two hundred warriors, a sixteenth-century report says, eight were gentlemen, the rest slaves. The implication of degradation was also transferred to the low kinds of labor. "In this hal," wrote Sir Thomas More (1551), "all vyle seruice, all slauerie . . . is done by bondemen."

It was in this sense that Negro servants were sometimes called slaves. But the same appellation was, in England, given to other non-English servants—to a Russian, for instance. In Europe and in the American colonies the term was, at various times and places, applied indiscriminately to Indians, mulattoes, and mestizos as well as to Negroes. For that matter, it applied also to white Englishmen. It thus commonly described the servitude of children. The poor planters complained, "Our children, the parents dieinge," are held as "slaues or drudges" for the discharge of their parents' debts. Penal servitude, too, was often referred to as slavery; and the phrase "slavish servant" turns up from time to time. Slavery had no meaning in law; at most it was a popular description of a low form of service. Yet in not much more than a half century after 1660 this term of derogation was transformed; it acquired a fixed legal meaning that described an entirely new condition of labor. In a society characterized by many degrees of unfreedom, the Negro fell into a status novel to English law, into an unknown condition toward which the colonists unsteadily moved, slavery in its eighteenth- and nineteenth-century form. The available accounts do not explain this development because they assume that this form of slavery was known from the start.

Can it be said, for instance, that the seventeenth-century Englishman might have discovered elsewhere an established institution, the archetype of slavery as it was ultimately defined, which seemed more advantageous than the defined British customs for use in the New World? The internationally recognized "slave trade" has been cited as such an institution. But when one notes that the Company of Royal Adventurers referred to their cargo as "Negers," "Negro-Servants," "Servants . . . from Africa," or "Negro Person," but rarely as slaves, it is not so clear that it had in view some unique or different status. And when one remembers that the transportation of Irish servants was also known as the "slave trade," then it is clear that those who sold and those who bought the Negro, if they troubled to consider legal status at all, still thought of him simply as a low servant.

Again, it has been assumed that Biblical and Roman law offered adequate precedent. But it did not seem to be so in the perspective of the contemporaries of the first planters, who saw in both the Biblical and Roman institutions simply the equivalents of their own more familiar forms of servitude. King James's translators rendered the word as "bondservant"; "slave" does not appear in their version. And to Coke the Roman *servus* was no more than the villein ("and this is hee which the civilians call servus").

Nor did the practice of contemporary Europeans fall outside the English conceptions of servitude. Since early in the fifteenth century the Portuguese had held Moors, white and black, in "slavery," at home, on the Atlantic islands, and in Brazil. Such servitude also existed in Spain and in Spanish America, where Negroes were eagerly imported to supply the perennial shortage of labor in the Caribbean sugar islands and the Peruvian mines. But what was the status of such slaves? They had certain property rights, were capable of contracting marriages, and were assured of the integrity of their families. Once baptized, it was almost a matter of course that they would become free; the right to manumission was practically a "contractual arrangement." And once free, they readily intermarried with their former masters. These were no chattels, devoid of personality. These were human beings whom chance had rendered unfree, a situation entirely comprehensible within the degrees of unfreedom familiar to the English colonist. Indeed, when Bodin (1606) wished to illustrate the condition of such "slaves," he referred to servants and apprentices in England and Scotland.

Finally, there is no basis for the assertion that such a colony as South Carolina simply adopted slavery from the French or British West Indies. To begin with, the labor system of those places was not yet fully evolved. Travelers from the mainland may have noted the advantages of Negro labor there, but they hardly thought of chattel slavery. The Barbadian gentlemen who proposed to come to South Carolina in 1663 thought of bringing "Negros and other servants." They spoke of "slaves" as did other Englishmen, as a low form of servant; the "weaker" servants to whom the concessions referred included "woemen, children & slaves." Clearly American slavery was no direct imitation of Biblical or Roman or Spanish or Portuguese or West Indian models. Whatever connections existed were established in the eighteenth and nineteenth centuries, when those who justified the emerging institution cast about for possible precedents wherever they might be found.

If chattel slavery was not present from the start, or adopted from elsewhere, it was also not a response to any inherent qualities that fitted the Negro for plantation labor. There has been a good deal of speculation as to the relative efficiency of free and slave, of Negro, white, and

Indian labor. Of necessity, estimates of which costs were
higher, which risks—through mortality, escape, and rebellion—greater are inconclusive. What is conclusive is the fact
that Virginia and Maryland planters in the seventeenth
century did not think Negro labor more desirable. A preference for white servants persisted even on the islands. But
when the Barbadians could not get them, repeated repre-
sentations in London made known their desire for Negroes.
No such demands came from the continental colonies. On
the contrary, the calls were for skilled white labor, with the
preference for those most like the first settlers and ranging
down from Scots and Welsh to Irish, French, and Italians.
Least desired were the unskilled, utterly strange Negroes.

It is quite clear, in fact, that as late as 1669 those who
thought of large-scale agriculture assumed it would be
manned not by Negroes but by white peasants under a condition of villenage. John Locke's constitutions for South
Carolina envisaged a hereditary group of servile "leetmen,"
and Lord Shaftsbury's signory on Locke Island in 1674 actually attempted to put that scheme into practice. The
holders of large estates in the Chesapeake colonies expressed no wish for a Negro labor supply, which they accepted only in the absence of an alternative. They could
hardly have planned to use black hands as a means of dis-
placing white. Restoration courtiers may indeed have
dreamed of setting up a new social order in America, and
Virginia and Maryland planters were no doubt eager to
lower costs, but the Negroes were not the instruments of a
plot to achieve those ends.

Yet the Negroes did cease to be servants and became
slaves, ceased to be men in whom masters held a proprie-
tary interest and became chattels, objects that were the
property of their owners. In that transformation originated
the Southern labor system.

Although the colonists assumed at the start that all servants would "fare alike in the colony," the social realities of
their situation early gave rise to differences of treatment.
It is not necessary to resort to racist assumptions to account
for such measures; these were simply the reactions of immigrants lost to the stability and security of home and

isolated in an immense wilderness in which threats from the unknown were all about them. Like the millions who would follow, these immigrants longed in the strangeness for the company of familiar men and singled out to be welcomed those who were most like themselves. So the measures regulating settlement spoke specifically in this period of differential treatment for various groups. From time to time regulations applied only to "those of our own nation," or to the French, the Dutch, the Italians, the Swiss, the Palatines, the Welsh, the Irish, or to combinations of the diverse nationalities drawn to these shores.

In the same way the colonists became aware of the differences between themselves and the African immigrants. The rudeness of the Negroes' manners, the strangeness of their languages, the difficulty of communicating to them English notions of morality and proper behavior occasioned sporadic laws to regulate their conduct. So Bermuda's law to restrain the insolencies of Negroes "who are servents" (that is, their inclination to run off with the pigs of others) was the same in kind as the legislation that the Irish should "straggle not night nor dai, as is too common with them." Until the 1660's the statutes on the Negroes were not at all unique. Nor did they add up to a decided trend.

But in the decade after 1660 far more significant differentiations with regard to term of service, relationship to Christianity, and disposal of children cut the Negro apart from all other servants and gave a new depth to his bondage.

In the early part of the century duration of service was of only slight importance. Certainly in England, where labor was more plentiful than the demand, expiration of a term had little meaning; the servant was free only to enter upon another term, while the master had always the choice of taking on the old or a new servitor. That situation obtained even in America as long as starvation was a real possibility. In 1621 it was noted that "vittles being scarce in the country noe man will tacke servants." As late as 1643 Lord Baltimore thought it better, if possible, to hire labor than to risk the burden of supporting servants through a long period. Under such conditions the number of years specified

in the indenture was not important, and if a servant had
no indenture, the question was certainly not likely to rise.

That accounts for the early references to unlimited service. Thus Sandy's plan for Virginia in 1618 spoke of
tenants-at-half assigned to the treasurer's office to "belong
to said office for ever." Again, those at Berkeley's Hundred were perpetual "after the manner of estates in England." Since perpetual in seventeenth-century law meant
that which had "not any set time expressly alloted for [its]
. . . continuance," such provisions are not surprising. Nor
is it surprising to find instances in the court records of
Negroes who seemed to serve forever. These were quite
compatible with the possibility of ultimate freedom. Thus
a Negro bought in 1644 "as a Slave for ever" nevertheless
was held "to serve as other Christian servants do" and was
freed after a term.

The question of length of service became critical when
the mounting value of labor eased the fear that servants
would be a drain on "vittles" and raised the expectation of
profit from their toil. Those eager to multiply the number
of available hands by stimulating immigration had not only
to overcome the reluctance of a prospective newcomer
faced with the trials of a sea journey, they had also to
counteract the widespread reports in England and Scotland
that servants were harshly treated and bound in perpetual
slavery.

To encourage immigration, therefore, the colonies embarked upon a line of legislation designed to improve servants' conditions and to enlarge the prospect of a meaningful release, a release that was not the start of a new period
of servitude, but of life as a freeman and landowner. Thus
Virginia, in 1642, discharged "publick tenants from their
servitudes, who, like one sort of villians anciently in England," were attached to the lands of the governor; and later
laws provided that no person was to "be adjudged to serve
the collonie hereafter." Most significant were the statutes
which reassured prospective newcomers by setting limits to
the terms of servants without indentures, in 1638–1639 in
Maryland, in 1642–1643 in Virginia. These acts seem to
have applied only to voluntary immigrants "of our own

nation." The Irish and other aliens, less desirable, at first received longer terms. But the realization that such discrimination retarded "the peopling of the country" led to an extension of the identical privilege to all Christians.

But the Negro never profited from these enactments. (The provision limiting the effectiveness of the act to Christians is not surprising in view of contemporary attitudes; thus another act of the same year excluded Quakers altogether.) Farthest removed from the English, least desired, the Negro communicated with no friends who might be deterred from following. Since his coming was involuntary, nothing that happened to him would increase or decrease his numbers. To raise the status of Europeans by shortening their terms would ultimately increase the available hands by inducing their compatriots to emigrate; to reduce the Negro's term would produce an immediate loss and no ultimate gain. By mid-century the servitude of Negroes seems generally lengthier than that of whites; and thereafter the consciousness dawns that the blacks will toil for the whole of their lives, not through any particular concern with their status, but simply by contrast with those whose years of labor are limited by statute. The legal position of the Negro is, however, still uncertain; it takes legislative action to settle that.

The Maryland House, complaining of that ambiguity, provoked the decisive measure. "All Negroes and other slaues," it was enacted, "shall serve Durante Vita." Virginia reached the same end more tortuously. An act of 1661 had assumed, in imposing penalties on runaways, that *some* Negroes served for life. The law of 1670 went further: "all servants not being christians" brought in by sea were declared slaves for life.

But slavery for life was still tenuous as long as the slave could extricate himself by baptism. The fact that Negroes were heathens had formerly justified their bondage, since infidels were "perpetual" enemies of Christians. It had followed that conversion was a way to freedom. Governor Archdale thus released the Spanish Indians captured to be sold as slaves to Jamaica when he learned they were Christians. As labor rose in value this presumption dissipated the zeal of masters for proselytizing. So that they be "freed from this doubt" a series of laws between 1667 and 1671 laid down the rule that conversion alone did not lead to a release from servitude. Thereafter manumission, which other servants could demand by right at the end of their terms, in the case of Negroes lay entirely within the discretion of the master.

A difference in the status of the offspring of Negro and white servants followed inevitably from the differentiation in the length of their terms. The problem of disposing of the issue of servants was at first general. Bastardy, prevalent to begin with and more frequent as the century advanced, deprived the master of his women's work and subjected him to the risk of their death. Furthermore, the parish was burdened with the support of the child. The usual procedure was to punish the offenders with fines or whippings and to compel the servant to serve beyond his time for the benefit of the parish and to recompense the injured master.

The general rule ceased to apply once the Negro was bound for life, for there was no means of extending his servitude. The most the outraged master could get was the child, a minimal measure of justice, somewhat tempered by the trouble of rearing the infant to an age of usefulness. The truly vexing problem was to decide on the proper course when one parent was free, for it was not certain whether the English law that the issue followed the state of the father would apply. Maryland, which adopted that rule in 1664, found that unscrupulous masters instigated intercourse between their Negro males and white females, which not only gave them the offspring, but, to boot, the service of the woman for the life of her husband. The solution in Virginia which followed the precedent of the bastardy laws and had the issue follow the mother seemed preferable and ultimately was adopted in Maryland and elsewhere.

By the last quarter of the seventeenth century one could distinguish clearly between the Negro slave who served for life and the servant for a period. But there was not yet a demarcation in personal terms; the servant was not yet a free man, nor the slave a chattel. As late as 1686 the words slave and servant could still be conflated to an extent that indicated men conceived of them as extensions of the same condition. A Frenchman in Virginia in that year noted, "There are degrees among the slaves brought here, for a Christian over 21 years of age cannot be held a slave more than five years, but the negroes and other infidels remain slaves all their lives."

It was the persistence of such conceptions that raised the fear that "noe free borne Christians will ever be induced to come over servants" without overwhelming assurance that there would be nothing slavish in their lot. After all, Pennsylvania and New York now gave the European newcomer a choice of destination. In Virginia and Maryland there was a determined effort to make immigration more attractive by further ameliorating the lot of European servants. The custom of the country undoubtedly moved more rapidly than the letter of the law. "Weake and Ignorant" juries on which former servants sat often decided cases against masters. But even the letter of the law showed a noticeable decline in the use of the death penalty and in the power of masters over men. By 1705, in some colonies, white servants were no longer transferable; they could not be whipped without a court order; and they were protected against the avaricious, unreasonable masters who attempted to force them into new contracts "some small tyme before the expiration of their tyme of service."

Meanwhile the condition of the Negro deteriorated. In these very years a startling growth in numbers complicated the problem. The Royal African Company was, to some extent, responsible, though its operations in the mainland colonies formed only a very minor part of its business. But the opening of Africa to free trade in 1698 inundated Virginia, Maryland, and South Carolina with new slaves. Under the pressure of policing these newcomers the regulation of Negroes actually grew harsher.

The early laws against runaways, against drunkenness, against carrying arms or trading without permission had applied penalties as heavy as death to all servants, Negroes and whites. But these regulations grew steadily less stringent in the case of white servants. Meanwhile fear of the growing number of slaves and uneasy suspicion of plots and conspiracies led to more stringent control of Negroes and a broad view of the master's power of discipline. Furthermore, the emerging difference in treatment was calculated to create a real division of interest between Negroes on the one hand and whites on the other. Servants who ran away in the company of slaves, for instance, were doubly punished, for the loss of their own time and for the time of the slaves, a provision that discouraged such joint ventures. Similarly Negroes, even when freed, retained some disciplinary links with their less fortunate fellows. The wardens, the equivalent of selectmen, continued to supervise their children; black men were not capable of holding white servants; and serious restrictions limited the number of manumissions.

The growth of the Negro population also heightened the old concern over sexual immorality and the conditions of marriage. The law had always recognized the interest of the lord in the marriage of his villein or neife and had frowned on the mixed marriage of free and unfree. Similarly it was inclined to hold that the marriage of any servant was a loss to the master, an "enormious offense" productive of much detriment "against the law of God," and therefore dependent on the consent of the master. Mixed marriages of free men and servants were regarded with particular disfavor as complicating status and were therefore limited by law.

There was no departure from these principles in the early cases of Negro-white relationships. Even the complicated laws of Maryland in 1664 and the manner of their enactment revealed no change in attitude. The marriage of blacks and whites was possible; what was important was the status of the partners and of their issue. It was to guard against the complications of status that the laws after 1691 forbade "spurious" or illegitimate mixed marriages of the slave and the free and punished violations with heavy penalties. Yet it was also significant that by then the prohibition was couched in terms not simply of slave and free man, but of Negro and white. Here was evidence in the policing regulations of an emerging demarcation.

The first settlers in Virginia had been concerned with the

difficulty of preserving the solidarity of the group under the disruptive effects of migration. They had been enjoined to "keepe to themselves," neither to "marry nor to give in marriage to the heathen, that are uncircumcised." But such resolutions were difficult to maintain and had gradually relaxed until the colonists included among "themselves" such groups as the Irish, once the objects of very general contempt. A common lot drew them together, and it was the absence of a common lot that drew these apart from the Negro. At the opening of the eighteenth century the black was not only set off by economic and legal status; he was, in the words a contemporary might use, "abominable," that is, another order of man.

Yet the ban on intermarriage did not rest on any principle of white racial purity, for many men contemplated with equanimity the prospect of amalgamation with the Indians. That did not happen, in many cases, for the mass of red men were free to recede into the interior, while those who remained sank into a slavery as abject as that of the blacks and intermarried with those whose fate they shared.

Color then emerged as the token of the slave status; the trace of color became the trace of slavery. It had not always been so; as late as the 1660's the law had not even a word to describe the children of mixed marriages. But two decades later the term mulatto is used; yet it does not serve, as in Brazil, to whiten the black, but to affiliate through the color tie the offspring of a spurious union with his inherited slavery. (The compiler of the Virginia laws then takes the liberty of altering the texts to bring earlier legislation into line with his own new notions.) Ultimately the complete judicial doctrine begins to show forth: a slave cannot be a white man, and every man of color is the descendant of a slave.

The rising wall dividing the legal status of the slave from that of the servant was buttressed by other developments which detracted from the qualities of the Negro as a human being, in order to establish his inferiority, and thus completed his separation from the white. The destruction of the black man's personality involved, for example, a peculiar style of designation. In the seventeenth century many immigrants in addition to the Africans—Swedes, Armenians, Jews—had brought no family names to America. By the eighteenth all but the Negroes had acquired them. In the seventeenth century Indians and Negroes bore names that were either an approximation of their original ones or similar to those of their masters—Diana, Jane, Frank, Juno, Anne, Maria, Jenny. In the eighteenth century slaves seem increasingly to receive classical or Biblical appellations, by analogy with Roman and Hebrew bondsmen. Deprivation by statute and usage of other civic rights, to vote, to testify, to bring suit, even if free, completed the process. And after 1700 appear the full slave codes, formal recognition that the Negroes are not governed by the laws of other men.

The identical steps that made the slave less a man made him more a chattel. All servants had once been reckoned property of a sort; a runaway was guilty of "stealth of one's self." Negroes were then no different from others. But every law that improved the condition of the white servant chipped away at the property element in his status. The growing emphasis upon the consent of the servant, upon the limits of his term, upon the obligations to him, and upon the conditional nature of his dependence steadily converted the relationship from an ownership to a contractual basis. None of these considerations applied to the Negro; on the contrary, considerations of consent and conditions disappeared from his life. What was left was his status as property—in most cases a chattel, though for special purposes real estate.

To this development there was a striking parallel in the Northern colonies. For none of the elements that conspired to create the slave was peculiar to the productive system of the South. The contact of dissimilar peoples in an economy in which labor was short and opportunity long was common to all American settlements. In New England and New York, too, there had early been an intense desire for cheap unfree hands, for "bond slaverie, villinage or Captivitie," whether it be white, Negro, or Indian. As in the South, the growth in the number of Negroes had been slow until the end of the seventeenth century. The Negroes were servants who, like other bondsmen, became free and owners of land. But there, too, police regulations, the rules of marriage, and the development of their status as property turned them into chattel slaves.

A difference would emerge in the course of the eighteenth century, not so much in the cities or in the Narragansett region, where there were substantial concentrations of blacks, but in the rural villages, where handfuls of Negroes were scattered under the easy oversight of town and church. There the slave would be treated as an individual, would become an equal, and acquire the rights of a human being. Men whose minds would be ever more preoccupied with conceptions of natural rights and personal dignity would find it difficult to except the Negro from their general rule.

But by the time the same preoccupations would fire men's imaginations in the South, the society in which the slave lived would so have changed that he would derive no advantage from the eighteenth-century speculations on the nature of human rights. Slavery had emerged in a society in which the unit of active agriculture was small and growing smaller; even the few large estates were operated by subdivision among tenants. After 1690, however, South Carolinians (and still later Georgians) turned from naval stores and the fur trade to the cultivation of rice, cotton, and indigo. In the production of these staples, which required substantial capital equipment, there was an advantage to large-scale operations. By then it was obvious which was the cheapest, most available, most exploitable labor supply. The immense profits from the tropical crops steadily sucked slaves in ever growing numbers into the plantation. With this extensive use, novel on the mainland, the price of slaves everywhere rose sharply, to the advantage of those who already held them. The prospect that the slaveowner would profit not only by the Negroes' labor but also by the rise in their unit value and by their probable increase through breeding accounted for the spread of the plantation to the older tobacco regions where large-scale production was not, as in the rice areas, necessarily an asset.

The new social and economic context impressed indelibly on the Negro the peculiar quality of chattel with which he had been left, as other servants escaped the general degradation that had originally been the common portion of all. Not only did the concentration of slaves in large numbers call for more rigid discipline; not only did the organization of the plantation with its separate quarters, hierarchy of overseers, and absentee owners widen the gulf between black and white; but the involvement of the whole Southern economy in plantation production created an effective interest against any change in status.

Therein the Southern mainland colonies also differed from those in the West Indies, where the same effective interest in keeping the black man debased was created without the prior definition of his status. The actual condition of the Negro differed from island to island, reflecting variations in the productive system, in the labor supply, and in economic trends. But with surprising uniformity the printed statutes and legislative compilations show no concern with the problems of defining the nature of his servitude. The relevant laws deal entirely with policing, as in the case of servants. A similar unconcern seems to have been characteristic of the French, for the most important aspects of the royal *Code noir* issued from Paris in 1685 were entirely disregarded.

The failure to define status may have been due, in the islands which changed hands, to contact with the Spaniards and to the confusion attendant upon changes of sovereignty. More likely it grew out of the manner in which the Negroes were introduced. Places like Barbados and St. Christopher were at the start quite similar to Virginia and Maryland, societies of small farmers, with a labor force of indentured servants and *engagées*. The Negroes and the sugar plantations appeared there somewhat earlier than on the continent because the Dutch, English, and French African companies, anxious to use the islands as entrepôts from which their cargoes would be re-exported to Latin America, advanced the credit not only for purchase of the blacks, but also for sugar-making equipment. But the limited land of the islands meant that the plantation owner and the yeoman competed for the same acres, and in the unequal competition the farmer was ultimately displaced.

The planter had no inveterate preference for the Negro, often, indeed, expressed a desire for white labor. But the limits to the available land also prevented him from holding out the only inducement that would attract servants with a choice—the prospect of landed freedom. From time to time desultory laws dealt with the term of service, but these showed no progression and had no consequences. The manumitted were free only to emigrate, if they could, or to hang about, hundreds of them "who have been out of their time for many years . . . [with] never a bit of fresh meat bestowed on them nor a dram of rum." The process of extending the rights of servants, which on the mainland was the means of defining the status of the slave, never took place on the islands.

The term "slave" in the West Indies was at the start as vague as in Virginia and Maryland; and when, toward mid-century, it narrowed down to the plantation Negroes as sugar took hold through the stimulus of the Africa traders, it does not seem to have comprehended more than the presumption of indefinite service. To Europeans any service on the islands continued to be slavery. For whatever distinctions might be drawn among the various groups of them, the slavish servants remained slavish servants. All labor was depressed, Negro and white, "domineered over and used like dogs." That undoubtedly affected emigration from the islands, the decline of white population, the relationships of blacks and whites, the ultimate connotation of the term slave, the similarities in practice to villenage, the savage treatment by masters and equally savage revolts against them, the impact of eighteenth-century humanitarianism, and the direction of emancipation.

The distinctive qualities of the Southern labor system were, then, not the simple products of the plantation. They were rather the complex outcome of a process by which the American environment broke down the traditional European conceptions of servitude. In that process the weight of the plantation had pinned down on the Negro the clearly defined status of a chattel, a status left him as other elements in the population achieved their liberation. When, therefore, Southerners in the eighteenth century came to think of the nature of the rights of man, they found it inconceivable that Negroes should participate in those rights. It was more in accord with the whole social setting to argue that the slaves could not share those rights because they were not fully men, or were at least a different kind of man. In fact, to the extent that Southerners ceased to think in terms of the seventeenth-century degrees of freedom, to the extent that they thought of liberty as whole, natural, and inalienable, they were forced to conclude that the slave was wholly unfree, wholly lacking in personality, wholly a chattel.

Only a few, like St. George Tucker and Thomas Jefferson, perceived that here were the roots of a horrible tragedy that would someday destroy them all. When the new nation came into being, the Negro and the connotation attached to his color proved a disturbing element to Americans who reflected on the significance of their own emergence as a people. Since slavery as an institution was not readily shaken off, it was necessary to justify the exploitation involved in it; and that led many earnest men along a line of thought few regarded with favor yet not many could resist.

CHAPTER II

One Blood or Many

ON THE eve of the Revolution, Americans were already preoccupied with the problems of their own nationality. The very designation American showed that they had become accustomed to thinking of themselves as one people; they were no longer simply Virginians or New Yorkers. It also reflected an inclination on their part to consider themselves distinct from the Englishmen and other Europeans who had been their ancestors. As Americans they were fond of describing themselves as new men, products of the New World environment in which they lived.

The logic of the debate with Great Britain and the revolutionary rhetoric of the 1770's heightened the sense of nationality. As they moved toward independence, the former colonists came to see their struggle in an ever widening perspective. They were fighting not simply to redress specific grievances, but also as a separate nation, to attain their own legitimate form of government.

The fact that the population of the United States had been derived from a variety of different sources was not an obstacle to the development of nationality or to the attainment of independence. Rather, precisely because their ancestors had not all been Englishmen, but also Dutch, Scots, Irish, Germans, and Swedes, the residents of the colonies had discovered a new identity as Americans. Subjection to the conditions of the new environment had molded them from many into one and had given them all a new, distinctive culture.

Confidence in the future course of American development rested upon a complex of assumptions about human
nature. The Judeo-Christian faith in the essential brotherhood of man under God implied that all humans were
ultimately descendants of the same pair of ancestors, and
that they shared common attributes. Whatever differences
distinguished types of men in the present, therefore, were
the products of historical development rather than of characteristics inherent to them. A system of psychology, derived from John Locke, accounted for the appearance of
national and racial differences. At birth the mind of man
was like a slate clean and unwritten upon; a succession of
impressions from without endowed it with social and cultural traits. The repetition of identical impressions from a
common environment in time produced the national characteristics of a people.

Therefore it was logical to believe that any kind of immigrant would, in time, come to conform to the common cultural pattern being shaped by conditions in the United
States. Ultimately the peculiar characteristics of Englishmen and Swedes and Germans would fade away and new
qualities derived from the New World would emerge.
Those new qualities would distinguish the Americans as a
group.

In the last quarter of the eighteenth century, however,
the Negroes already seemed an uncomfortable exception
to this rule. From the start enormous cultural differences
had separated them from the white colonists, and in the
eighteenth century the slave status had shaped those differences into an unbridgeable gulf. The logic of their innermost beliefs drove white Americans to make the effort to
conceive that ultimately the Negroes, too, would be like
them and that black and white would somehow become
one people. And men fighting for their own rights faced
an obligation to show they were animated by "a general
philanthropy for all mankind, of whatever climate, language, or complexion." With the people of Darien, Georgia,
they were compelled to declare their "disapprobation
and abhorrence of the unnatural practice of Slavery in

America." But uncomfortable realities stood in the way of action upon such beliefs.

In the North the problem was not so pressing. Less than ten per cent of the Negroes in the United States lived in New England and the Middle States, where slavery was in the process of disappearing. In the rural regions Negroes were gaining gradual acceptance and were occasionally intermarrying with whites. In the cities, where the numbers were larger, the Negroes were a group apart, but they enjoyed a defined role and status; and there were grounds for hope that, given time, they would merge with other Americans of the same class and situation. Dr. Benjamin Rush gave characteristic expression to white expectations. He explained that the blackness of the Negro must have been due to a great disease that had once swept across Africa and hoped that life in the United States would ultimately remedy these unfortunates and permit their absorption in American society.

The South could not afford such easy optimism. The number of its Negroes was too great, and despite more than a century of residence in the New World these Negroes had scarcely begun to approach the whites among whom they lived. Slavery was a tragic barrier the awareness of which could not be effaced, nor could the sense of bitterness it had generated be easily overcome. In his *Notes on Virginia*, Jefferson voiced the trepidation that many Southerners felt: whatever the future of slavery, contacts between whites and blacks would remain uneasy. The violence of the great Negro revolts in the French West Indies gave point to these fears. Early in the new century St. George Tucker was explaining that a major social disaster would follow emancipation, however necessary that might be.

Such was the unhappy reality. How was a Southern American to explain it? It was not enough to argue with John Drayton (1802) that nature had made "some to be poor, and others to be rich; some to be happy and others to be miserable; some to be slaves and others to be free." More generally, the South, like the North, acknowledged the injustice of slavery and recognized the obligation to end the institution. Furthermore, in the three decades after the

Revolution, this form of bondage was not profitable. The old tobacco plantations were languishing as their owners struggled with the burden of supporting numerous Negroes whose labor was not worth the cost of feeding them. There seemed no reason to perpetuate an institution so thoroughly out of keeping with the needs and ideals of the new society.

Only Southerners were inclined to doubt that even as a free man the Negro could take his place as an equal in the society that had once held him a slave. Deep-rooted prejudices held by the whites and "ten thousand recollections by the blacks" would cause endless disorders. Then, too, were not the Negroes different, in their color, in their moral and emotional character? Perhaps, "whether originally a distinct race, or made distinct by time," they were "inferior to the whites in the endowments both of body and mind." Jefferson advanced that speculation "as a suspicion only," since "they have never yet been viewed by us as subjects of natural history." An uneasy suspicion certainly, if Americans were a nation in the sense that they thought they were.

As the eighteenth century drew to a close, a similar question was being asked with regard to the red men, who were, after all, the first Americans. There had been a time when the belief had been comfortably expressed that the Indians too would merge with the new settlers. There seemed no logical obstacles to such a development, toward which devoted missionaries long had labored. The Indians had been subject longest to the American environment, and presumably would follow a course that other Americans would also take. Indeed, this accounted for Jefferson's great interest in the Indian culture and his impassioned defense of their character. Not nature but circumstance had retarded their civilization, which for the moment stood in the situation of the Germanic tribes when contact with the Romans stimulated their genius.

But toward the end of the century there were disturbing indications that this anticipated development was not actually taking place. For decades the Indians and the white settlers had been bitter rivals; the long series of savage wars had left memories that could not readily be downed. Everywhere the red men had been resented as uncomfortable obstacles in the way of expansion. Even in 1820 they would still stand athwart the frontier in Georgia, Alabama, Mississippi, and Indiana.

What was more, the Indians had not, in time, shown the inclination to adopt the standards of civilization accepted by other Americans. They refused to fall into settled ways of life; they rejected the learning of books; and they were slow to find the faith toward which the missionaries urged them. Contact with the whites seemed only to deprive the Indians of their primitive virtues. A dismaying series of reports to the Massachusetts Historical Society in the 1790's described the degeneracy of many tribes as they succumbed to the settlers' influence. Vice, intemperance, and disease were the products of such associations. In the face of this evidence the belief that the red men would ultimately share the nationality of the whites was difficult to maintain.

But to surrender that belief called for a major intellectual accommodation. Already some Americans were attempting to explain the special case of the Indians. The tribes, some urged, were separate and independent nations occupying a portion of the continent, but not properly a part of the United States. They could not therefore be expected to merge with the Americans.

This argument flew in the face of actuality. Americans, in practice, did not acknowledge the sovereignty of the Indian in his territory. As individuals, and through their government, they consistently assumed the right of final decision despite the elaborate pretense of formal treaties and conferences with the red men. It could be argued, indeed, that the Indians were, in a manner of speaking, wards of the United States, which exercised on their behalf powers they could not exercise for themselves. But that was a lame argument, one not altogether convincing even to those who used it. In any case, the assertion that the Indians were still separate nations did not account for the small groups of them sprinkled throughout the Eastern states, completely ruled by the whites among whom they lived, and yet not a part of American society.

There was no explanation. The Indians, like the Negroes,

were enclaves in the nation, disturbing and irritating groups the existence of which contradicted the fundamental American assumptions as to the nature of man.

Nevertheless, few Americans were disposed to surrender the faith in the conception of nationality that held them together. Stubbornly, perhaps irrationally, they clung to the general doctrines of human brotherhood and equality, of natural rights, and of the capacity of men to reshape themselves and their environment. The problems of the intractable Negro and Indian were left to wishful daydreams in which miraculously the bothersome enclaves disappeared by themselves. The certainty of American progress was an opiate; someday the injustices of slavery would vanish and the Indians would be pacified. And then the white society would find itself disembarrassed of its red and black elements.

Perhaps they would move away. If only these disturbing peoples might be persuaded to migrate, that would contribute to the relief of all concerned. After all, to the west the whole continent lay open. Why should they not move toward the opportunities there? Or to Mexico, where St. George Tucker suggested the Negroes would find more suitable homes? Or to the Pacific, where the North Carolina legislature requested Congress to reserve territory for emancipated "persons of colour"? Most attractive of all was the suggestion that the black men, once freed, might be induced to return to the homes of their ancestors in Africa. The pathetic delusion that the Negroes after generations of life in America would be able to settle in Liberia led scores of conscientious Southerners to support the efforts of the American Colonization Society. The hope that the future would somehow of itself solve the problem permitted Americans to push to the backs of their minds the contradiction between their fundamental conceptions of nationality and the existence of the Negro and Indian enclaves.

After 1820 that hope gradually died under the pressure of new views of slavery and new conditions in the West. In the four decades prior to the Civil War a vast outpouring of white settlers, native- and foreign-born, spilled across the empty lands to the Mississippi and beyond. Thriving farms and busy cities dotted the whole interior region; and state after state came into being, totally engulfing the islands of residual Indians. In some places little reservations of red men remained, and beyond the Mississippi extensive tracts were still designated as Indian Territory. But few Americans of this period doubted that they would ultimately spread across the whole continent and take possession of these lands also. What would happen to the Indians when there was at last no West to which they could be pushed?

Nor did the hopes for Negro removal approach any closer to realization in the decades after 1820. The experiment in Liberia dragged on, with little success. As year after year went by, the faith faded that this might be a solution. The difficulties and the costs of removal now seemed hopelessly high. Then, too, slavery was ceasing to be a burden in the South and became instead immensely profitable. Cotton culture developed as the interior regions opened up to settlement and as the expanding textile industry in old and New England created an ever larger market for the king of crops. Even Virginia and Maryland, which did not themselves raise cotton, gained by the increased value of the slaves whom they exported to the new plantations of the black belt.

Indeed, slavery was not retreating but expanding. Decade by decade the lands in bondage grew more extensive with the westward spread of the plantation. No longer could the well-intentioned imagine that the problems of the Negroes any more than those of the Indians would gradually disappear of themselves.

In the face of this challenge many Americans clutched at the straws of indecision. Unwilling to accept the responsibilities of commitment, they resolutely shut their eyes to the very existence of the problems. Yet it was not possible always to escape the demands of self-interest, or the necessities of political decision, or the obligations of reason and morality. Slowly two distinct attitudes toward the Negro and the Indian were defined; and the difference in situation

unhappily identified one attitude with the North, the other
with the South.

In the North, and particularly in New England, the old
beliefs were pressed to their ultimate conclusion. The Indian was to be treated as an equal, relieved of the burden
of wardship, and steadily assimilated with the whites. By
the same reasoning the Negro was to be emancipated and
led toward equality. Here the problem involved few difficulties. The handfuls of red and black men were no threat
to the social order. Furthermore, a religious imperative supported these views. For the Quakers and the evangelistic
sects slavery was a sin, to be rooted out if the whole society
were to be saved. Together with men who believed in a
secular progress they joined in the ranks of the abolition
movement.

In the South it was more complicated. As slavery grew
more profitable and the number of blacks increased, the
imposing problem of the Negro grew more serious. The
sense of guilt of Jefferson's generation persisted, but the
intellectual burden of it grew more painful.

The new circumstances made it hard to conceive of the
disappearance of slavery, even at some remote future date;
and without that consoling assurance the Southerners could
not bear to acknowledge that their society harbored within
it an ineradicable evil. The only alternative was to deny
that slavery was an evil.

Down to the 1840's Southerners were still able to charge
that slavery was a "moral and political evil," a "mildew
which has blighted . . . every region it has touched." But
the guilt was too heavy longer to bear. Abolitionists became
unpopular and were compelled to be silent or to move
away. Their wild talk disturbed "the quiet and content-
ment of the slave," who "becomes the midnight murderer
to gain that fatal freedom whose blessings he does not comprehend." As pernicious in their threats to order were the
free Negroes; the outbreaks by Vesey in 1822 and Turner
in 1831 seemed to prove the necessity of repression. Slavery
had now to be defended as a permanent feature of Southern life.

As the attacks upon slavery mounted in bitterness, many

Southerners adopted a posture of resentful defensiveness. Not slavery but its critics were responsible for the plight of the Negro. The institution, one could prove, was amply recognized by the Constitution and sanctioned by the law. It had had a place in every polity and was justified by classical .as well as by Biblical precedent. It strengthened the religious and the moral order; Chancellor Harper of South Carolina pointed out that the white prostitutes of Europe and the North had no place in the South and that there was a virtue to licentiousness that did not affect the women of one's own class. Then again slavery was politically necessary. Without this means of assuring internal peace and stability society would be rent asunder by "eternal and inveterate struggles" and "a deadly war of extermination" would put an end to democracy.

What was more, slavery was essential to the well-being of the whole economy. It was manifestly vital to the prosperity of the South; abolition, no matter how effected, would turn the region into a desert. But Northern mills and Western farms, linked to the plantations below the Mason-Dixon Line, would also suffer in the absence of a servile labor force. And even the Negro was the gainer from his bondage. He had been raised from barbarism to a state of security, if not of comfort. Slavery had taught him the ways of civilization; without it he might be reduced to the destitution of the wage slaves in Northern factories. Notoriously the free Negroes were "the most worthless and indolent" elements in society. The deterioration of the Negroes in Canada and the West Indies after emancipation was an indication of the unpleasant fate that might befall the slave were he deprived of the shelter of beneficent bondage.

Such were the interminable arguments of half-convinced men. The weary search for precedent, the laborious interpretation of texts, the accumulation of questionable facts persuaded only those who wished to believe. Furthermore, this whole line of thought flew in the face of Christian and of the democratic tradition, and it threatened all the lower elements in Southern society. The majority of whites who were not slaveholders were not, after all, altogether ready to acquiesce in a view of society in which the plantation was the ideal. They were likely to wonder, as Hinton Helper ultimately did, what effect slavery had upon those who were neither masters nor slaves. Always the discussion came back to a central dilemma: how did bondage square with freedom?

It was attractive, therefore, to seek to resolve that dilemma with the idea that slavery was "not a national evil" but, on the contrary, "a national benefit," a positive good, and one particularly appropriate for the Negroes as a group. Experience taught that mankind was divided "into grades," the "mutual dependence and relations" of which constituted "the very soul of civilization." If there were sordid, servile, and laborious offices to be performed, asked Chancellor Harper, was it not "better that there should be sordid, servile and laborious beings to perform them?" It was only necessary to discover the "infallible marks" by which individuals of inferior intellect and character could be selected at birth to know who was fit to labor at such tasks in the interests of the whole society.

Such marks were evident in the distinctive traits of the Negro. He had been blackened, J. J. Flournoy asserted, by "some dispensation from on high," no doubt as a punishment; and the defect in color was matched by defects in character—indifference to liberty, of which he had no conception but "that of idleness and sloth," the lack of affections, and low intelligence. Some of these qualities were physical, related to anatomical differences which, according to S. A. Cartwright, permitted him to live with less oxygen, to resist tropical diseases, and to labor under conditions whites could not endure. The Negro, "with molasses blood sluggishly circulating . . . nose broad and flat . . . mind and body dull and slothful . . . will weak, wanting or subdued," was the complete opposite of the red-blooded, brilliant-eyed, strong-willed white. For the blackness of the Negroes was "not confined to the skin," but pervaded "the whole inward man down to the bones themselves, giving the flesh and the blood, the membranes and every organ and part of the body, except the bones, a darker hue." But even those qualities which were accidental, "however acquired in the first instance," were transmitted "unimpaired

to their posterity for an infinite succession of generations."
The Negroes, said Thomas Dew, had been made slaves not
by law, but by their own nature. Declare them free and you
"depress, instead of elevating them." In actuality, explained
President Elliot of Planters' College, Mississippi, the term
slave in America meant not a kind of servant, but "the
African race."

Here was the formula to purge the guilt of men who believed in liberty but were the masters of slaves. If only they
could bring themselves to use it, by taking the final step
to the assertion that the Negroes were not really human
but another species, then under slavery, all *men* would be
free and equal.

There was, however, a striking reluctance to take that last
step; only a tiny radical minority did so as yet. The great
majority of Southern whites could describe the blacks as
the descendants of Cain or of Canaan, or of Ham; but they
could not escape the Christian doctrine of a single ultimate
progenitor created in the image of God. They could not
admit, any more than could the *Southern Quarterly Review*
(1855), that they held their slaves "only as a higher race
of Ourangs, not really contemplated in the authoritative precepts on which the morality of Christendom is
founded." To have done so, the Richmond *Enquirer* explained, would have been to destroy the Bible and lay bare
"the very citadel of our strength to our foes."

Furthermore, so long as slavery was a legally recognized
status, there was a profound ambiguity in its defense. Some
Southerners were not satisfied to argue only that slavery was
desirable as a condition for the Negro; they were tempted
also to vindicate the institution "in the abstract, and in the
general, as a normal, natural, and *in general*, necessitous
element of civilized society, without regard to race or color."
It was "as much in the order of nature that men should enslave each other, as that other animals should prey upon
each other."

But to argue that no culture could exist without slavery,
nor republican institutions survive in its absence, confused
the statement of position insofar as it was intended to justify the inferiority of the Negro. Implicit in the theories of

Fitzhugh and the other defenders of slavery as a general good was the corollary that if the Negroes had not been available for bondage some other group would have been found. "If slavery is a blessing," Henry Clay proclaimed in 1838, "the more of it the better and it is immaterial . . . whether the slaves be black or white." What then was the relevance of the traits that made the blacks inferior? The conception of the Negroes as a race was thus hopelessly confused with that of their status as slaves, and that confusion would persist in the South until the Civil War ironically resolved it.

The same difficulty intruded in another way into Southern thinking about the Indian, who was free yet colored. Untainted by the inferiority of the slave status, the red man was often endowed by the white with a reputation for primitive virtues—courage, love of freedom, and a concept of honor, for example. He enjoyed the same presumption of freedom as the whites, and contacts along the frontier had permitted some degree of marriage and miscegenation.

Yet the Southern defender of slavery could not conceive that the Indians would someday take a place in his own society. So long as the tribes held desirable lands east of the Mississippi they set an intolerable obstacle in the way of expansion and at the same time created a disruptive refuge for fugitive Negroes; only by a move to the Far West could they yet hope to save themselves. As important, their redness was a problem for those who argued that color was a trait indicative of the inferiority of the group. In the 1830's T. R. Dew was already reasoning that the Indians should have been enslaved and that a greater number "would have been saved, had we rigidly persevered in enslaving them." As it was, their future was dim; the further advance of settlement would ultimately lead to their extermination. Only slavery could save them from the consequences of their inferiority.

The destruction of slavery through the Civil War removed the ambiguities in the Negro's position. After emancipation the law recognized no status but freedom; there were to be no serious efforts to restore the old forms of bondage. If differences among individuals and groups were still to be maintained, they had to be justified on some other ground. If the inferiority of the Negro was still to be asserted, it could not be on the basis of his condition as slave, but only on the basis of his race.

The improvement in his position therefore proved temporary. The spread of racist ideas, unforeseen by the emancipators of 1865, soon consumed the fruits of liberation.

The same ideas made total assimilation the only alternative to total separation, and that ultimately had a deleterious effect upon all other people of color.

In the North and in some parts of the South the war strengthened the abolitionist ideal for a time. Those who had formerly labored for the Negro's freedom on humanitarian grounds now conceived it their task to labor also for his complete equality. The reality was still remote from the ideal. Even in the strongholds of antislavery sentiment the blacks suffered from economic and social discrimination. But down to the end of the century their situation improved steadily and the ultimate objective of the total assimilation of all groups with one another remained attractive.

That philosophy was also relevant to the Indians. Their difficulties, it was argued, derived from their position of wardship and dependency, which discouraged initiative and thrift and deprived them of individual title to their lands, "the chief incentive to labor and exertion—the very mainspring on which the prosperity of a people depends." In retrospect their removal to the West appeared a mistake. In the East they would have been compelled to acquire the civilized qualities of the whites.

To make all the Indians at once citizens of the United States would be a grotesque blunder. But that was the desirable goal toward which policy ought to be directed. Meanwhile their reservations were blocks in the way of civilization that ought to be divided and sold for their own benefit. The Dawes Severalty Act of 1887 was a first step towards destroying the tribalism that kept the Indians apart and inferior.

Until that date the same assumption was generally applied in the North to all the groups in, or on their way to, America. Even those citizens who had begun to consider the desirability of restricting immigration had, as yet, no doubts as to the nation's ability to assimilate the newcomers already arrived.

The dominant reaction in the South was altogether different. For two decades or so after the war the situation of the freed slaves improved perceptibly. But soon those who resisted the new trend, for whatever reason, found they could call upon the aid of powerful emotional brakes to halt the advance toward equality.

The majority of the whites would under no circumstances yield their position of superiority. To accept the equality of the Negro would have run counter to the complex of beliefs and habits nurtured through almost two centuries of slavery. It would also have amounted to an admission of guilt, not only for the injustices of slavery, but also for the disaster of war. That was intolerable. The inferiority of the Negro was more than a habit of thought, more than a justification for privilege. It was an article of faith, made necessary by the society's history.

White superiority could no longer be maintained by the legally established slave status. But it would be maintained, and in the last quarter of the nineteenth century the means were forged for doing so. White superiority was now to be supported by a fixed pattern of relationships between the former masters and the former slaves. The two groups were to remain apart and every contact—social, political, and economic—was to recognize and affirm the continuing inferiority of blacks to whites.

A comprehensive doctrine of race was essential to justify the developing patterns of segregation. The Negroes were a separate, distinct, biologically inferior species and that explained their degradation despite the futile effort to bestow freedom and equality upon them by law. Furthermore, reiteration of this argument was necessary through the whole nation. The white South was but a minority, and it needed to secure the acquiescence of the North in the abandonment of the rights guaranteed the Negro by the Thirteenth,

Fourteenth, and Fifteenth Amendments. It was essential to have the facts of Negro inferiority "widely circulated" to show that any questioning of God's wisdom in creating race differences was "blasphemous." If the "social contact of race" was "contrary to natural laws," it was as injurious "on one side of the Mason-Dixon Line as on the other."

The influence of these ideas could be measured in the successive judicial decisions which gradually accepted the premises of the Southern position and recognized the permanence of "racial instincts." By the end of the century the impact of the racist conceptions, even in the North, had led to a widespread revision of judgments as to the history and prospects of the Negro in America. His past slavery and present inferiority were regarded as necessary products of his essential difference as a human being from the white.

The penetrating power of the racist ideas derived from the circumstance that they were by now capable of being applied under other conditions in other parts of the Union.

The Chinese on the Pacific coast had, at first, been welcome for their labor's sake. By contrast with the Negro they were "clean, orderly, and industrious," obedient, "affectionate, and grateful." Such "a race could *fully* blend with" the whites.

After 1873, however, these model newcomers aroused the increasingly bitter antagonism of influential white groups and were stigmatized for their color. They, too, it was argued, were racially separate and unable to mingle on terms of equality with the Caucasians. Their low character, lack of moral sense, and criminal instincts made their exclusion imperative, or, at the very least, demanded that they be kept firmly subjected in an inferior status. The same accusations, later, would be leveled against the Japanese and other Orientals.

Indeed, the idea proved extraordinarily pliable; in a variety of situations presumed racial differences could be made to justify the exploitation of, or discrimination against, helpless groups. Often in the last decade of the century the Indians were denounced as skulking brutal savages pampered by sentimental humanitarians. The imperialists who urged a policy of rapid overseas expansion upon the United States insisted that the white race had the right and duty to rule over inferior peoples. The mission of America was no longer simply to extend the blessings of free institutions to all men, but rather to govern those whom racial inferiority made incapable of self-government. "Now that the United States has embarked in imperial enterprises," wrote Professor J. W. Burgess in 1902, "the North is learning every day by valuable experiences that there are vast differences in political capacity between the races, and that it is the white man's mission . . . to hold the reins of political power in his own hands for the civilization of the world."

By the end of the century the pattern of racist practices and ideas seemed fully developed: the Orientals were to be totally excluded; the Negroes were to live in a segregated enclave; the Indians were to be confined to reservations as permanent wards of the nation; and all whites were expected to assimilate as rapidly as possible to a common standard. Only by then it had also become clear that the racial lines could not be drawn simply on the basis of color. Some Americans had long wondered, for instance, that "although the Jewish race has been subjected . . . to every possible variety of . . . moral and physical influences in the four quarters of the earth, yet, in *no instance*, has it lost its own type or approximated to that of other races." And as the volume of immigration went up, speculation increased as to whether there were not among whites equally important racial distinctions that set the newcomers off from the native Americans.

There were, of course, Americans who dissented from what had become the dominant view. Such men insisted on interpreting their nationality "irrespective of race differences." The old conceptions of equality and brotherhood, of diversity as a higher form of unity still held the faith of many individuals and groups. Charles W. Eliot, for instance, stubbornly insisted on the cultural value of differences; and there were always the committed idealists ready to defend the rights of the underprivileged.

But the influence of those who insisted that the Slavs, the Jews, the Japanese, and the Negroes were fully Americans waned as the racist ideas grew consistently stronger. By the opening of the twentieth century those who stood by the old conception of nationality were already using the terms of argument of their opponents. That was a sign of the impending victory of the conception that man was not of one blood, but of many.

The development of these ideas in the United States had historically been associated with the exploitation of dependent forms of labor. "You are made to hate each other," Tom Watson once said, "because upon that hatred is rested the keystone of the arch of financial despotism which enslaves you." Significantly that association could be found in other parts of the world too—in Africa, in Asia, in Europe itself—as dominant groups strove to keep large populations of laborers in permanent subjection.

But does recognition of that association imply that racism was simply the product of exploitation? A fuller examination of that question in the United States and elsewhere will reveal that there were other sources for the concept of "white supremacy" and of the racial inferiority of other peoples.

CHAPTER III

Prejudice and Capitalist Exploitation

THE APPEAL to prejudice to justify the exploitation of a dependent group was not peculiar to the United States. Illustrations of the same deceptive use of racism are abundant in other parts of the world.

Yet to proceed from that fact to the conclusion that exploitation causes prejudice is a misleading oversimplification. In the years just after the Second World War, when the defeat of nazism seemed to have opened the way to solution of all these problems, there was a superficial plausibility to that conclusion. The prestige of the Marxist view of the class struggle and the delusion that all race conflicts had disappeared in the Soviet Union seemed to confirm the analysis that economic disorders were at the roots of prejudice. It will be necessary to examine critically certain ideas derived from that oversimplified belief.

Three significant books published between 1946 and 1948 present striking statements of the conception of group prejudice as a social disease produced by capitalism. Two of the volumes deal with the Jews, the third with the Negroes, the two racial groups who were the victims of social hatred in our times. These books offer an opportunity for the comparison of the phenomenon in the United States and elsewhere. Finally, the three works have in common an identical conception of the nature of the disease; all found it the product of exploitation in Western capitalist society.

Perhaps more than any other writer of his time, Carey McWilliams made popular the cause of America's "minorities" and exposed the dangers that lie in all the manifestations of prejudice. He possessed a quick and easy pen; he had a knack for assimilating scholarly opinions and making them readable; and he had strong opinions—on the whole, good ones.

A *Mask for Privilege* (1948) was, however, one of his weaker efforts. It labored under the burden of an untenable thesis and was all too often careless in matters of detail.

The key to the book was its title. For Mr. McWilliams, anti-Semitism in the United States was always a "mask for privilege." The development of industrialism between 1860 and 1877 left patent injustices in the structure of American society. By the latter year "the industrial bourgeoisie had triumphed." Once triumphant, "the industrial tycoons discovered that they could not function within the framework of the social and political ideals of the early Republic. To insure their triumph, a new social order had to be established." That new order involved the creation of a status system to protect the position of the privileged classes. "To trick a freedom-loving people into accepting industrial regimentation in the name of democracy, the tycoons of the period needed a diversionary issue." They therefore devised a countertradition to oppose the democratic tradition, and they based that countertradition on the myth of anti-Semitism, first applying it in the social, then in the economic, and finally, in recent times, in the political sphere. A pattern of exclusion, established first in resorts, clubs, and colleges, restricted the opportunities open to Jews and drove them into marginal occupations. As capitalism approached its crisis, concentration in undesirable trades left the Jews in an exposed position, increasingly open to attack by fascist groups like the anti-Semitic Columbians, who were making trouble in Georgia in 1947.

To prove his position McWilliams had to argue that a single line of development generated anti-Semitism in the United States. He therefore assumed throughout that all anti-Semitic forces grew up indigenously within the country. On the level of ideology he failed to treat the influence from abroad of the works of Gobineau, Lapouge, Drumont, and Chamberlain. On the practical level he did not mention the impact of German government propaganda in the 1930's through such agencies as the Friends of New Germany, the German-American Bund, and George Sylvester Viereck.

Again, since he felt compelled to attribute the whole to the activities of the "tycoons," he consistently slurred over the influence of liberal thinkers tainted with anti-Semitic ideas. Yet in the total development Edward A. Ross and John R. Commons, who were well-intentioned reformers, but who popularized racist conceptions, probably had a wider effect than did outright champions of "Aryanism" like Madison Grant and Lothrop Stoddard. Bolstered by the prestige of academic reputation, of affiliation with worthy causes, and of good intentions, the books of the liberals were doubly dangerous because they did not carry the poison labels of the openly biased.

Similarly McWilliams disregarded the part played by organized farmers and laborers in the anti-Semitic movements. There is not a reference to the fact that populist hatred of Wall Street sometimes fell into the anti-Semitic pattern. There is no recognition of the fact that trade unions also adopted exclusionist practices. No more vicious racist ideas were ever expressed than those spewed out by Samuel Gompers in the A.F. of L. campaign against the Chinese. If these same ideas were ultimately used against the Jews, that only illustrated further the complexity of the subject and the dangers of oversimplification.

The necessities of its thesis led *A Mask for Privilege* to the erroneous proposition that the position of the Jews as objects of prejudice was unique in American society. McWilliams could not make clear, for example, that the prejudiced comments he quoted were often directed against all new immigrants and not only against Jews. One would never learn from his book that Americans of Irish descent experienced the same difficulties as Jews in penetrating the elite social clubs, that the sons of Italian parents also faced quota barriers when they sought admission to medical and dental schools, and that the Ku Klux Klan between 1920 and 1928 was decidedly more hostile to Catholics than to Jews. Until the 1930's, indeed, there was no anti-Semitic movement in the United States that was not also anti-Catholic.

To support the contention that the Jews occupied a unique position in America, McWilliams argued that they had been crowded, by prejudice, into a marginal and insecure role in the nation's economy: they were excessively concentrated in the professional and white-collar occupations; they engaged in consumption and in distribution rather than in basic production, in light rather than in heavy industry. He viewed the anomalous position of the Jews as basically due to their forced adjustment to exclusion from the more desirable places in the economy. Anti-Semitic bias, he pointed out, "more than any other single factor . . . has brought about the peculiar distribution of Jews on the checkerboard of our economic system."

This line of reasoning rested upon two fallacious suppositions: first, that Jews could have gotten the most desirable places had they not been thus handicapped; and second, that the conception of what were the most desirable places was the same among all people. To McWilliams the facts that only thirty-three of the four hundred and twenty directors of New York banks were Jews, that only three of the mass-circulation magazines were owned by them, and that in "not a single sector of the heavy industry front" did their influence "amount to dominance or control" were evidences of discrimination. But it could just as well—or just as badly—be argued, in view of the recency of Jewish settlement and in view of the poverty of the Jews when they arrived, that to produce almost ten per cent of the bank directors in the financial capital of the nation was evidence of a *lack* of discrimination. Certainly the representation in banking and in heavy industry of other groups descended from recent immigrants was no larger.

Conclusive evidence on this point could be drawn from the situation in agriculture. The American farm was individually owned. Prejudice could bar from this occupation no one who had the capital, and for more than half a century a melancholy succession of unsuccessful organizations

stood ready to provide Jews with the capital. If Jews did
not become tillers of the soil in America, it was not because they could not, but because they would not. That
indicated that such groups had their own occupational
preferences.

Finally, McWilliams depended entirely upon the power
of coincidence to explain the beginnings of anti-Semitism,
and he endowed the American capitalists with amazing
foresight in relating social to economic discrimination.
Joseph Seligman, a prominent Jewish banker, was excluded
from a Saratoga hotel in 1877, the year of the triumph of
the industrial bourgeoisie. That this "first overt manifestation of anti-Semitism in the United States took place in
1877 is to be explained," McWilliams held, "in terms of
the corrosion which the industrial revolution had brought
about in the American scheme of values." That American
values were so instantly and automatically corroded was itself rather farfetched. More important, this explanation
implied that those who excluded Seligman envisaged and
consciously planned the subsequent development of the
status system and of the pattern of economic discrimination
that emerged thirty years later. This rational conspiracy,
simple and all-embracing, was dubious on the face of it
and did not square with the character of American capitalists at the turn of the century. But without such a conspiracy there was a fatal gap in McWilliams's argument.

The idea of economic marginality, applied in *A Mask
for Privilege* to the American scene, was earlier applied by
some thinkers to the role of the Jews in the European economy. Dov Ber Borochov, for one, believed that a normal
distribution of occupations took the form of a pyramid,
with the great mass of the population concentrated in agriculture and in the heavy industries and tapering off in
numbers through distribution, light industry, trade, and
the professions. In the case of the Jews the pyramid was
reversed, and their difficulties were ascribed to the fact that
they lacked the security of a proper base in the productive
system. This theory accounted for the great effort by progressive Jewish leadership to "productivize" the Jews of

eastern Europe, and was also at the root of certain elements of Zionist ideology.

The questions of how and why this situation came to exist were usually skirted. McWilliams, too, passed the questions by with the comment that they were interesting but irrelevant. But the importance of the problem did not escape the attention of a young Polish Jew who spent most of his short life in Belgium. As a member of Hashomer Hatzair—a left-wing Zionist group—Abram Léon absorbed Borochov's interpretation of the Jewish situation, and his awareness of the problem was certainly sharpened during the war, when he became a member of the section of the anti-German underground allied with the Fourth International. Actively engaged in the resistance movement, he nevertheless found time to compose a shrewd analysis of the historical sources of the Jewish economic position, and had just about finished this book when he was arrested. In Auschwitz, at the age of twenty-six, he met the fate of millions of his fellows.

Léon's approach was that of the orthodox Marxist. His analysis, despite errors of detail, was a solid statement of the materialistic interpretation of the Jewish question. Its bias was evident. But its thoughtfulness and originality were nonetheless stimulating.

Running through two and a half millenniums of the Jewish past, Léon found two points of crisis in the secular history of that people. The first crisis occurred when the economy of the Roman Empire broke down and gave way to the kind of natural economy associated in western Europe with feudalism, a mode of production characterized by self-sufficient agriculture and the absence of commerce. This transformation coincided with the emergence, as state religions, first of Christianity and then of Islam. Léon believed that these developments set in motion a selective process that froze the Jews in commerce: that is, the settled Jewish farmers tended to be absorbed by the dominant creeds, and only those continued to adhere to Judaism who had the relative independence of the trader's status.

At this stage, Léon continued, a rigid and exceptional occupational pattern was fixed upon the Jews. In the long period until the thirteenth century, while the whole of Europe lived by agriculture, the Jews engaged in itinerant trade. And since all those with whom the Jews dealt were self-sufficient, that commerce of necessity centered largely on the importation of luxuries and catered to the tastes of the nobility, who alone had the surpluses to pay for them. Of necessity also the Jews engaged in usury to finance the feudal lords in the frequent intervals when the manors failed to produce sufficient surplus. Naturally the status of the Jews was high and they enjoyed the protection of the highly placed.

This relatively pleasant situation began to change in the era of the Crusades. The natural economy disintegrated as exchange developed. But now commerce and mercantile capital were directly connected with production; the objects of trade were no longer exotic luxuries, but the products of industry. (The famous Italian banking houses, for instance, established themselves in the woolen business.)

The Jewish merchants, unable to enter the new commerce, were gradually excluded from all trade. Consequently they were compelled to live by usury and by its ancillary occupations, pawnbrokering and dealing in second-hand goods. In this role they battened off the nobility and off the townspeople, who ultimately became their bitter enemies. For a time the sovereign, who profited by extorting the wealth of his subjects through the Jews, offered some protection. But in the end the hostility of the new middle class and the gentry led to harsh measures, to the growth of the ghetto, and finally to exclusion. A remnant of Jews saved themselves only by migrating eastward to Poland and Bohemia, less developed regions still in the natural-economy stage.

Thereafter the Jews hung on in the west on a very marginal basis until the end of the eighteenth century, when emancipation loosed the old restrictions and assimilative forces began steadily to absorb the new citizens into the sprouting national states. But at that very moment the position of the eastern Jews, which had been quite favorable until then, began to deteriorate through the workings of the same forces which had operated in the west several centuries earlier. In Poland and in Russia a new middle class rising from the disintegration of the old economy was jealous of the place of the Jews in commerce and in the professions. Competition for status led to political restrictions upon the Jews and to emigration to France, Germany, and England, which only worsened the position of their co-religionists in the west.

At this point the internal contradictions of capitalism deprived the Jews, a marginal group at best, of the last vestiges of security. Excluded from the cartels of the great capitalists, the Jews were driven into speculation, a development which offered the monopolists an opportunity to divert the discontent of the masses to the Jews alone. Theorists began to distinguish between "bad" (speculative) capital and "useful" (productive) capital, terms which Nazi economists eventually translated into parasitic-Jewish and productive-national. Ultimately the masses fell subject to a new ideology which identified speculative capitalism with Judaism and contrasted it with a planned national socialist economy, which was really war capitalism. Under the successive blows of persecution in the name of this ideology the Jews were helpless and took refuge in a nationalism of their own.

By this survey Léon attempted to demonstrate that the Jewish question was the outcome of an identification of the Jewish group, through definite historical circumstances, with certain limited occupations which the rest of the society found inferior or degrading or hostile. Anti-Semitism then could readily be understood as a device consciously contrived by the capitalists for their own end.

The questions raised in specific form by Léon with reference to the Jews were essentially the same as those treated a few years later by Oliver Cromwell Cox (*Race, Class and Caste*) in a more general way; basically both men were concerned with the phenomena of caste, class, and race, and of the relationships among them. Unfortunately Mr. Cox's enormously prolix volume, winner of the George Washington Carver award, fell far short of its goal of definitive analysis.

The book was cluttered with the deceptive paraphernalia of scholarship. But through it ran a very simple thesis, a product of the confused years in which it was written; and that thesis must be understood before the mazes of argument can be unraveled. The following quotations will make clear the author's point of view and will also throw light upon his methods. In a discussion of the modern state Cox wrote, "From the standpoint of degrees of development of democracy in the three great nations of the world . . . the United States is probably most backward and Russia farthest advanced." Of the New Deal he wrote, "Most of what [Franklin Roosevelt] said and did was really democratic and consequently socialistic or communistic." In other words, Cox was then taken in by the pervasive identification of all social ills with capitalism, of all social advances with socialism.

These sentences also illustrate this author's peculiar use of language; words were divorced from their usual meanings and endowed with esoteric connotations appropriate to a closed system of thought. In the fantastic sequences of seeming inaccuracies it was hard to differentiate between what was only double talk and what was really error of fact. The reader could decide for himself. Thus the Hindus "never attained a conception of nationality." There is only one political party in the United States, "with two factions: Republicans and Democrats." Mercantilism is state capitalism. A ruling class is always intolerant. "Businessmen constitute our ruling class." Democracy "is in fact communism." De Tocqueville was an advocate of democracy. "The bourgeosie is unalterably opposed to democracy." Russia is the only foe of fascism; most respectable Americans are fascists; Southern poor whites are not hostile to the Negro; the late Senator Bilbo was a spokesman of capitalism. And no previous scholars revealed these truths because their "bread and butter" depended upon "avoiding the study of contemporary class conflict."

Beyond these semantic diversions lay the central thesis: Cox viewed racial antagonism as one of the fundamental traits of the class struggle within the capitalist system. Prejudice was, to his mind, an attitude built up by the capitalists to keep control over the proletariat, whom they exploited.

The point was made in a long, tortuous argument complicated by Mr. Cox's difficulty in defining race in such a way as to take in the Negroes in the United States and not much more. What finally emerged, however, was somewhat broader than that. For if a race was "any group of people that is generally believed to be, and generally accepted as, a race in any given area of ethnic competition," then the Chinese in California, the Jews in Nazi Germany, the Italians in Australia, the Mexicans in Texas, and the French Canadians in Maine were also races.

But many of the groups just named found their most prejudiced persecutors not among the capitalists. Cox therefore had to reason that any antagonisms not inspired by the capitalists, despite his definition, were not really race conflicts. He disposed thus of the anti-Oriental movement on the Pacific coast, which—inconveniently—was led by workingmen, indeed by the trade unions. Likewise, the Jews who faced hostility even before the rise of capitalism were, he said, never victims of race prejudice, only of intolerance.

Similarly, to demonstrate that racial antagonism could not exist without capitalism, a long section of the book was devoted to demolishing the thesis that the caste system of India was a product of precapitalist color prejudices. Cox's refutation is convincing, although his own explanation of the causes is open to question. At the same time he seized the occasion to lay a basis for comparison between the idyllic Hindus and the horrid capitalists. He managed, for example, to overlook the terrible punishments meted out to violators of the caste laws and thus found no violence in the caste system; in his view the depressed portions of society, there, by persuasion, happily granted privileges to their superiors.

Having tied race prejudice to Western capitalism, Cox proceeded to show, by another ingenious exercise in terminology, that prejudice was an aspect of the class struggle inherent in capitalism. He created an entity, the "political class," which, by definition, was a "power group" struggling for control of the state. In his own day, then, there were two political classes, the challengers of the *status quo* and its defenders, the proletariat and the bourgeoisie, the communists and the non-communists.

Cox did not trouble to relate his "political class" to any social or economic groupings that could be shown actually to exist in the real world and which he variously denominated "estate," "social class," and "functional class." Consequently he found no difficulty in emerging with the conclusion that there could be no solution to prejudice short of the violent overthrow of the capitalist system by revolution, which, in view of the premises and of the methods employed, was not altogether suprising.

What was surprising was how close this position brought the author to the racist's own picture of race relations. Like the most reactionary white Southerner, although for different reasons, Mr. Cox argued that laws against lynching must necessarily be ineffective, that there could be no contact between races without either conflict or amalgamation, and that whites acted as a unit in opposition to blacks.

For all the differences among them these three books had a basic element in common: all regarded prejudice as an instrument used by capitalists to justify or to increase exploitation.

Such a theory must pass the test of one crucial question: why should one group rather than another have been selected as the object of prejudice? And, indeed, each of the three books, in its own fashion and to some degree, attempts to demonstrate that an occupational peculiarity in the group singled out rendered it particularly appropriate for its role as object of the exploiter's prejudice. For Cox the problem was simple. The Negro had been a slave; he remained an oppressed worker. Hence the odium attached to him as an inferior human being.

But the case of the Jew was more difficult. Insofar as McWilliams confronted this problem, his solution was essentially the same as that of Abram Léon: that concentration in certain marginal employments left the Jews vulnerable. But the mere fact that Jews clustered in certain callings could not explain the appearance of racist anti-

Semitism. Faith in such an explanation rested on the questionable assumption that some occupations were, of their nature, undesirable. The distinction between productive and unproductive trades sometimes made by economists —Marxist as well as orthodox—has not been one that greatly influenced popular values; witness the attitudes toward movie stars and athletes. In modern times, at least, people have measured the agreeableness and the utility of any employment by the yardsticks of income and status, and if Jewish callings seemed less desirable than others, it is because they somehow fell short in terms of those criteria.

So far as income was concerned, there seem to have been no disabilities connected with Jewish occupations; no one ever charged that Jews made too little money. But inferiority of status was undoubtedly attached to trades that were distinctively Jewish. That inferiority was not, however, inherent in the occupations involved. On the contrary, it arose from the fact that Jews pre-empted certain trades; these were "Jewish businesses." The Jews were not held in low repute because they engaged in callings intrinsically disreputable. Rather those callings lost esteem because the Jews were identified with them.

Most important of all, concentration in a limited number of occupations was characteristic of all ethnic groups and not simply of those, like the Jews and the Negroes, who suffered from prejudice. Some, like the Quakers in the United States and the Scots in England, to name only two, displayed a markedly eccentric occupational pattern and still attained an exceptionally high social status. In European and American society there always remained a kind of hereditary element in occupation as in every other aspect of culture; skill, training, values, and opportunities were, to some extent, handed down from father to son even in the most fluid economies. No ethnic group was normal, because normality in this sense could only be an average of many ethnic groups.

But if Western society comprehended a multitude of ethnic groups, all differentiated to some degree in economic structure, then prejudice could not be explained simply in terms of exploitation. Why should the exploiter have directed his prejudice against one group rather than another? Neither McWilliams nor Léon could, in these terms, explain why the Jews should have been the "chosen people." And Mr. Cox could not explain why seventeenth-century Americans bore the same prejudice against both white and black servants.

Nor was there any accounting for the difference in tastes of the capitalists of other countries. Why should the Brazilians and Frenchmen not have picked on the Negroes? Why should color have been a bar to a Hindu in India but not in England? Why should capitalist prejudice anywhere not have taken a quite different form?

These are important questions. They cannot be answered simply by reference to the fact that race prejudice has often been used to justify the exploitation of men by their masters. Economic exploitation was somehow involved; in the experience of the American Negro in slavery the link certainly existed. And in other societies, too, race hatred has been a device of oppression, of political rivalry, and of national aggression. There is evidence enough that, in some way, exploitation, an expression of economic or political maladjustment, meshed in with race prejudice. The difficulty is to define the relationship.

A clue to the solution is the fact that exploitation created a sense of social uneasiness in which there was room for, and psychological and political unity in, prejudiced behavior. A society weighed down by such uneasiness found relief by dividing against itself: in other words, by sanctioning the hatreds of some of its members against others. Those individuals most disturbed in personality or situation yielded most readily. But as attacks from without or depression or political crisis exacerbated uneasiness, the impulse to seek such relief became more universal and more compelling and the cathartic hatreds more intense. Not the fringes alone, but society as a whole was affected.

Such hatreds were, of course, not always oriented along ethnic lines. Sometimes people held prejudices against "Reds" and "unions," against "capitalists" and "Wall Street." But when that bias took an ethnic direction, it acquired a special depth and an entirely different quality.

To comprehend that depth and quality it is necessary to recognize the fact that race prejudice rested upon a system of beliefs and drew into play the innermost emotions of man. An understanding of those beliefs and emotions will reveal the characteristics that made race an instrument of exploitation in Western society.

Prejudice as Idea and Emotion

CHAPTER IV

The Linnaean Web

RACISM embodied a series of intellectual propositions. To whatever uses these ideas were put and whatever the cruel perspective of history may say as to their consequences, they grew out of truth-seeking explorations into the nature of man and of human society.

There was a lad in Sweden who dreamed of order and who could not keep his mind on his studies. To the despair of his father, Carl Linnaeus showed no inclination for the life of a clergyman. In 1726, when Carl was already nineteen, there seemed no alternative but to apprentice him to the shoemaker.

The local doctor interceded; in his employ Carl began to fit some meaning to his random interest in nature. In pursuit of that meaning he shortly went off to the university, where he studied after a fashion and also lectured, and whence he now and again set off on long journeys. More than a decade passed and he earned a degree in medicine. But he had no desire to spend his life in dosing and bleeding.

Much later a title of nobility would change his name to Carl von Linné and he would be honored throughout the Western world. But his early years he spent in the hand-to-mouth poverty of the dependent scholar. It did not matter, for he lived mostly in a self-enclosed world, absorbed in the examination of the endless variety of nature. There were so many plants, for instance, each individual and different! Yet as he probed their inmost character, measured and matched stamens and pistils, the variations were not random, but orderly and meaningful. He sought the meaning.

A meaning had to be there. Nature was not a chance agglomeration of beings and things. It had been designed by its Creator in accordance with a plan, and its mechanism functioned with a regularity that was law. Every least object in it had a purpose, and in all were made manifest the intentions of the Divine Architect who had first put them in motion. If one could but seize the proper clues, they would reveal still further the meaning of the universe that Newton and Leibnitz had already begun to explore. Such were the dreams of a young man curiously peering beyond the many-hued petals of his flowers.

But how was order to be made of all this diversity? Certainly the first step was to establish the relationship among the bewildering multitude of organisms sprinkled by the bounty of nature across the globe. "Each and every species which has been created by God should be properly distinguished and recognized, both of earths and stones, of plants and trees, of insects, fishes, birds, and all other animals." In this task the observation of Leibnitz was helpful: there was a continuing hierarchy of beings from the lowest to the highest among those that inhabited the earth. But the general assumption to which that observation gave expression only reflected the faith that such an order existed. It did not itself describe the order.

To describe that order was Linnaeus's achievement. In 1735 he published *Systema Naturae*, the system of nature. Painstakingly he had put the fragments into place by creating a system that would hold them all, type by type, each in the variations of its species and genera. Among the other animals located near the ape was man. Successive editions in the years that followed elaborated and refined the scheme, for the work aroused immediate and continuing interest. It supplied the gap between the general assumption that an order existed in nature and the specific observations of travelers and scientists. What had been needed, and what Linnaeus supplied, was a mode of classification that would arrange the data of nature in a form from which generalizations could be drawn. For more than a century thereafter the task of classification would occupy scholars. Meanwhile Linnaeus had spun a web in which generations of unhappy thinkers would be trapped.

Linnaeus himself had distinguished four variations among men, based on differences in color. Buffon and others soon added depth and detail to his categories of animals.

It is not surprising that those who wished to create a science of man and of society should regard an analogous categorization of peoples as a first step. Montesquieu showed that laws and customs varied from nation to nation. Did it not follow that to uncover the underlying principles of such variation it was first necessary to classify the types of men for whom the laws were made? As the boundaries of the known world fell away, the Europeans were exposed to the rich diversity of humanity. Travelers brought back exciting accounts of Russia and China; Africa and America offered strange and provocative details; from Australia and the South Seas came conflicting and contradictory data. If this wealth of information could but be ordered and classified, what secrets of man and society might it not reveal!

Through the eighteenth century—and well into the nineteenth—the prevailing view of human history and the accepted doctrines of Christian faith set the limits within which science established such classifications. Man's experience on earth was a continuous story, with a definite beginning and a foreseeable end, and with a regular progression from the one to the other. In this universal drama—whether conceived in theological or secular terms—all men were participants. When the Abbé Raynal, in 1776, attempted to account for the rise and fall of civilizations, or when Condorcet, fifteen years later, attempted to justify the faith in indefinite progress toward perfectibility, they did so by describing a single unending stream of history in which the peoples of all times and places had parts.

By the same token the Biblical account of a single creation with all men equally the descendants of Adam prejudged the weight that could be given to racial differences. An occasional venturesome, and eccentric, thinker like

Lord Kames speculated on the possibility of polygenesis, that is, of a number of acts of creation from which were derived the varieties of mankind. But this notion was so clearly contrary to revelation as to carry no weight. Always the central problem was defined in another way: given the common ancestors of man, how could one account for the actual visual physical dissimilarities among types of men?

The usual answer was that the differences had appeared through degeneration, a term then used without unfavorable connotation. The children of common ancestors had slowly altered their characteristics as they spread to the various environments on the earth's surface. Perhaps, as Immanuel Kant explained, there were latent, in the original parents of all, diverse potentialities that were developed as external conditions encouraged them. That would explain why the members of the different races nevertheless belonged to the same species and were thus capable of mating with one another.

In order to understand how the various races originated and developed from a common source, it was necessary to delineate these groupings distinctly. Only thus could the modes of descent be comprehended. This task occupied natural scientists for three quarters of a century after 1776. Kant, like Linnaeus, had made out four grand divisions based on color, which was presumed to have some relationship to climate. But color alone soon seemed inadequate as a criterion, and a succession of industrious scholars proceeded to refine the means by which differences could be recognized. Camper, for instance, attempted to assess the significance of the "facial angle" as a criterion.

A more significant approach was that of Blumenbach at the close of the eighteenth century. He stressed the importance of head shape in his definition of five human races. Only it was difficult to set up a scheme for classifying the infinite variety of human heads. After 1830 it nevertheless seemed increasingly important to do so, for Spurzheim, Gall, and the scientists of phrenology were proving that the physical attributes of the cranium corresponded to the qualities of the human mind and character.

At last, in 1842, Anders Retzius hit upon the appropriate

device. From the Belgian Quételet he had learned that statistical measurements could be used to describe average types. Now Retzius invented the cranial index, a precise number, derived from measurements of the head, which classified individuals in their appropriate races. It was no longer necessary to deal simply in the gross categories of color; the more exact terms of head shape were also available as clues to the development of the variations in mankind.

In the interim other scholars had fashioned additional tools of identification. The idea that social and physical traits were closely related had stimulated interest in the knowledge of language. The process of classification so useful in natural history could also apply to human history. Grammarians, philologists, and students of folklore diligently peered into the roots of words, as the botanists did of plants, in the effort to make out the family ties that would expose the secrets of derivation from a common source.

In Germany, Franz Bopp applied immense learning to the problem. French and Italian had manifestly a common parentage. But as he studied roots and inflections and traced the permutation of consonants, he discovered connections between them and German, between ancient Latin and Greek. Clearly the linkages revealed a common descent from a single ancestral language. And if there once was a single tongue, parental to the great languages of Europe, did that not mean that there had once been a single race to use that tongue? The learned men ventured even to speculate upon the character of those unknown people, whom they called the Aryans.

The identical logic led to the conclusion that the other languages of men must have had their sources in other distinct races; the Arabs, the Chinese, the Indians, the Africans were surviving representatives of people who had spoken the ancient Hamitic, Dravidian, Semitic, and other vanished equivalents of the Aryan Sanskrit. In addition the expanding fund of historical information supplied a wealth of material for the exercise of scholarly imaginations. Thus the deciphering of the hieroglyphics touched off a chain of inquiry into the character of the ancient Egyptians, into the nature of their civilization and the causes of its decline.

It seemed reasonable, of course, to try to make the linguistic families coincide with the physical races described by the natural scientists. Linguistics became, as it were, a branch of anthropology. No doubt the Aryans of the philologists were the same white-skinned, long-headed Caucasians the natural historians had already come to define; just as Renan's pure Semites were undoubtedly round-skulled and swarthy. If actual observation of the men and women who walked the streets of Paris and London and Berlin did not confirm the theory, that could readily be explained. Centuries of contact with other races had mixed extraneous elements into the original strain. The men of the mid-nineteenth century could draw upon an extensive literature, in which history and myth were inextricably mingled, that identified the various elements of Europe's tribal past; Celts and Saxons, Gauls and Teutons, Goths and Romans were summoned into service to account for the ancestral development of the Europeans.

These earnest speculations found eager readers in the United States; clearly they were relevant to the situation of a nation which numbered among its population large groups of Negroes and Indians as well as the diverse immigrant folk. "It was true," insisted Dr. Henry S. Patterson, that "the management of these folk depended in a great measure upon their intrinsic race-character." But inquiries parallel to those pursued in Europe developed only slowly across the Atlantic. The predominant concern of Old World scientists had been to show the origin of the different nationalities of the present in a common racial source. Americans were more interested in the process by which people of diverse origins coalesced in a common nationality; and they had faith in the capacity of their country to assimilate any variety of man. In the United States, therefore, the absence of a common national ancestry and confidence in the assimilating influence of the environment as yet inhibited the line of thought that emphasized inherent differences among the races of men. Furthermore, there was no corps of indigenous scientists free to pursue such investigations; theological influences were still over-whelmingly powerful in the colleges and that certainly dis-couraged departures from traditional beliefs. Only a hand-ful of physicians, at once independent and interested in science, were able to turn their thoughts to these problems.

Such a doctor made his rounds in Philadelphia in the 1830's. It could hardly be said that Samuel G. Morton was outstandingly successful at his profession. Yet he was emi-nently well qualified. Reared in a Quaker community, he had had the opportunity to study in the famous medical school at Edinburgh and to travel on the continent. When he came back to Philadelphia he was as well trained as any American. But his mind was on other matters.

In Europe he had learned the theories of the phrenolo-gists and the anthropologists, had been persuaded of the importance of the body in shaping the mental and moral attributes of men. Blumenbach's distinctions were of course familiar to him, and, once back in America, he longed to extend man's knowledge of this important, and neglected, subject. Yet when he prepared to deliver a lec-ture in 1830 he discovered he could not, in Philadelphia, even lay his hands on the proper skulls to illustrate the differences among the Mongolian, the Malay, and the Caucasian.

Skulls became his life's work. He industriously set to work assembling cabinets of craniums and studied their measurements with devotion. He exchanged views with scholars occupied in similar studies and, from Gliddon, the American consul in Egypt, he secured specimens and in-formation on the ancient races. (The Negroid appearance of the Sphinx was deceptive. What seemed to be "woolly hair" was only "his wig," and the Ramses family was "quite Caucasian.") Laboriously Morton extended the older clas-sifications, dividing the races into distinct families, and his work won the approbation of the famous Retzius himself.

Always, however, he ran into the stone wall of the Bibli-cal account of creation. To his private journal he expressed uneasy doubts, but he had no wish to disturb the faith of others. Yet how was it possible to explain the manifest physical differences among men if all were equally the offspring of a single pair of parents? It was not adequate to point to the Noachian flood; the sons of the patriarch were three in number—not enough for the five races—and there was still the problem of their common parentage. Nor would the fanciful accounts of other catastrophes hold water in the face of geological evidence.

Cautiously Morton advanced the idea of a multiple creation. Dr. Charles Caldwell had already pointed out that the Biblical chronology left too short an interval between the fall of man and the beginning of known history to permit the radical changes in the human constitution essential if the Negro and the white European really were offspring of the same ancestors. But, Morton wondered, had the Scriptures actually said that they were? The author of the Pentateuch had described the lives of Adam and Eve. But had he really excluded the possibility that elsewhere on earth, outside the Garden of Eden, there were other beings from whom the non-Caucasians might have descended? There was no connection between the Old World and the New of the existence of which the Bible was not even aware; the American Indians, therefore, must have been separately created.

Decisive in Morton's mind was his ability at last to surmount one long-standing scientific obstacle. It had generally been believed that different species could not mate with one another and continue to generate offspring. The ability, therefore, of men of every variety to intermarry had been accepted as proof of the unity of the human species. Morton, however, discovered "a latent power of hybridity . . . in many animals in the wild state" so that unlike species could crossbreed and remain prolific. "Consequently the mere fact that the several races of mankind produce with each other a more or less prolific progeny" constituted "no proof of the unity of the human species." Then "the doctrine of the original diversity of mankind" unfolded itself to him "more and more with the distinctness of revelation."

One of his correspondents, Dr. Josiah C. Nott of Alabama, had also been troubled by the problem of crossbreeding. But he could see all about him evidence that the mulatto was a "degenerate, unnatural offspring" of disparate parents. Therefore, like Morton, he concluded that "the human race is descended from several or many original pairs," placed by an all-wise Creator in the climate and situation best suited to their peculiar constitutions. As for the Negro, he was no nearer to the white man than to the ape.

These suggestions evoked outraged protests from the defenders of tradition. Not even the fact that the great Louis Agassiz seemed persuaded earned them acceptance. The Swiss naturalist had not been sure when he had come to the United States in 1846. He knew, even then, that different types of men flourished in different faunal-floral provinces. But did that mean that they differed in origin? Contact with the Negro and the arguments of Nott and Morton in the next five years convinced him the answer was yes. Few other Americans, however, were yet willing to accept that answer. Scientists had gone a long way, in Europe and in America, in classifying humanity into its various branches; but they still insisted all had one root. With the learned Prichard they affirmed "all human races are of one species and one family." The certainty of a single ultimate progenitor remained; and the notion of plurality passed into the limbo of eccentric hypotheses that were echoed in no popular response.

Only a handful of men, perplexed but stubborn, insisted that Morton's problem was real and still unsolved. The differences among the races must be located in some secret difference in their origin.

In the second half of the century the problem in Europe and in America took on an altogether new aspect. The traditional conception of human history disintegrated; Darwin decisively altered man's appraisal of the operations of nature; and mounting tension in the contacts of white with colored people prepared the ground for the view that mankind was permanently divided into distinct races, biologically separate from one another. The decisive scientific discoveries and theoretical formulations were made in the Old World. But their influence quickly extended across the Atlantic.

At mid-century the framework of Biblical chronology was already shattered. A generation of scholarship had de-destroyed the belief in the literal accuracy of the sacred texts. It was possible still to cling to them as poetic meta-phors, but they were no longer regarded by the learned as capable of contradicting what geology taught as to the age of the earth, what anthropology revealed as to the length of man's experience on earth, and what history described as the variety of civilizations through which man had passed. Adrift from the once firm moorings of the Bible, scholars of every degree of competence allowed their minds to range through the countless eons of the past in search of a meaning for the present.

Among the young men who lived through the reign of Louis Philippe in France there were some for whom the passing years conspired only to bring frustration. Their memories were crowded with the borrowed recollections of glory. Idle reveries drifted readily back to the chivalric images of bold men acting without restraint, of passions gratified without inhibition, of achievements easily recog-nized in immediate consequences. Alas, these were figures of a past contained in books and legend; the dismal present had no equivalent. In the stolid bourgeois world all was covered over with mediocrity and convention. The crowded rows of flats and little houses had engulfed the splendid monuments of the past; and the swarming little men to whom power had fallen, gross and incapable of dreaming, nevertheless in their mass stifled the dreams of their betters.

What were the dreamers to do as the century approached and passed its mid-point? They were not willing, under Louis Philippe, to play for the petty stakes of the favored desk in the bureaucracy. Nor would they admire the pan-dering to a revolutionary mob by which Napoleon III crept upon his throne; they cherished enough standards of good taste to keep them apart from the circus atmosphere of the Second Empire's court. Dreams were better. But they needed justification.

That was the plight of Count Arthur de Gobineau. Out-wardly a studious young man, fastidious but devoted to his books, he burned for a distinction his society did not recognize. Later he would discover for himself a Viking ancestor, Ottar-Jarl, a fierce northerner, ruthless in his integrity, who would have swept away with his sword the fripperies and falsities of the boulevards. Now Gobineau met with a little group of his fellows in a society they called the Scelti, the chosen ones, where they despised the masses who did not recognize them as their fathers' sons.

At the least he could find an explanation for the tragedy that had deprived him of his proper role. For, in the morass of its unlovely creations, the nineteenth century had produced one worthwhile pursuit—science—from which the universe kept no secrets. Knowledge might not forestall the decay of the future, but it ennobled those who possessed it.

Gobineau's *Essai sur l'inégalité des races humaines* (1853) was a history, but one strong in its certainty of the known fact, for it rested firmly on all the scientific learning of his time. The opening chapters were given over to an exposition of the laws of nature which revealed that races differed from one another in their physical beauty, in their cultural power, and in their spiritual capacity, as well as in language and body structure. The work then reached back to the dawn of man's experience, where it discovered the earth divided among the black, yellow, and white races. Successive chapters traced the relationships among those races in detail, for in those relationships was hidden the cause of the rise and fall of civilization.

The story stretched over thousands of years. The white Aryans, in India, Egypt, Greece, and Rome, and finally the West, had always displayed power, energy, and the ability to lead. Contact with other races had spurred them to the creation of civilizations, in which they were invariably the upper caste. But always the inferior blood of the lesser races had acquired a numerical preponderance which led inevitably to degeneration. (Now the term has decidedly an unfavorable connotation.) In particular, the Semites had time and again injected Negro strains into the dominant race and thus enfeebled it beyond the power of recovery. The moral for the nineteenth century was inescapable.

In widening circles through the next four decades the

book found readers and admirers. It influenced the thought of Wagner and Nietzsche. Its implications were spelled out in histories of politics and art and literature. Its terminology and concepts crept into best-selling novels and popular poetry.

In America, Gobineau's work was received with particular enthusiasm by the friends and collaborators of Dr. Morton. Charles D. Meigs, who had a few years earlier written a sympathetic memoir of the craniologist, was an obstetrician accustomed to regarding the French as in the forefront of scientific development. Josiah Nott, in Alabama, was at that very moment collaborating with another of Morton's correspondents, G. R. Gliddon, in a study of the types of mankind designed to prove that the races were indeed distinct and unchangeable. Here in Gobineau's learned volumes was indeed corroboration of a most convincing sort. In 1856 a translation appeared in Philadelphia with a supplementary note by Nott on the scientific validity of the Frenchman's theories. In the years that followed, these ideas gained steadily in relevance as the problems of the Negro, of the Indians, of the immigrants, and of imperialism more often troubled the nation.

But even before the decade was over, they were to be immeasurably strengthened by a revolutionary change in the scientific foundation on which they rested. For Gobineau the origin and purpose of the different races was a mystery, the product of God's inscrutable will. It would not remain a mystery long.

Appropriately enough the public exposition came at the July 1 meeting of the Linnean Society in 1858. This was the work of another of those dreamers who had half-heartedly resisted a father's desire to shunt him into the ministry. Charles Darwin's youth had also an aimless quality, manifest in his unwillingness to focus his energies or his powers of observation within any circumscribed limits. Intoxicated with nature, he could not cut any part of it out of a continuum in which the lowliest clod, the glistening coral, the earth-bound plant, the barnacle, the worm, even man himself, were a part.

He took them all in, in a kind of detached love that demanded that he find for each its relationship to the whole. To show that plants were capable of moving or that the action of worms formed vegetable mold was to add to the dignity of their being. The restless probing of his mind sought a total understanding of nature, and he was singularly fortunate, in his long lifetime, to arrive at a conception that quickly earned almost universal assent among scientists in every discipline.

For those concerned with the study of the races of mankind Darwin's theory of evolution resolved the problems that for a century had been their stumbling block. No longer was it necessary to worry about the descent of men from a unique pair of ancestors divinely created at a single point in time. The idea of natural selection made it possible to think of creation as a process. The species were not immutable. They had developed, and the visible differences among the races could be interpreted as evidence of differences in the capacity to survive.

Furthermore, Darwin, in the love of nature, had argued there was a community of descent from animal to man. He had thus destroyed the belief in the uniqueness of humanity and also the belief in its homogeneity. For if the similarities among mammals were as numerous as *The Descent of Man* made out, then the resemblance of the Caucasian to the Negro might be no more significant than the resemblance of either to the ape.

Finally, Darwinism helped to destroy the conception of history as a drama moving from a known beginning to a foreseeable end, with man its central actor. The universe of nature, it appeared, was indifferent to men, creatures thrown up by an impersonal process that had existed eons before their appearance and that might go on for millenniums after they had joined the extinct species of earlier ages. The mind could hardly conceive the variety of possibilities the evolution of the future might take. Nor could it fully comprehend the sources from which the real differences among human beings had sprung. But it could now understand the plurality of the human race.

The task of the scientist was to explore the operations of

evolution; and the first step, now more important than ever, was that described by Linnaeus: to put order into the mass by arranging individuals in their proper categories. The purpose of the arrangement, however, was no longer that of discovering the common characteristics of unchanging species. Rather, classification became an inductive science that was to show the natural relationship of forms in the sense of descent by evolution.

Now was the time when the ruler and calipers came into their own. Scores of measurers attacked the human frame, seeking precision in the indexes that would distinguish one breed from another. The new anthropological societies co-ordinated the efforts of research. Paul Broca and others outdid themselves in devising ingenious instruments—a process that reached its culmination in A. von Török's achievement, five thousand measurements on a single skull. The systems became more detailed and more rigid, and the various orders of man were set in place among the different races.

As the century drew to a close, the task became more pressing. The classifications were more necessary, for they were being put to use in a variety of unexpected ways. In 1869 Sir Francis Galton's studies of the heredity of genius seemed to prove that many cultural as well as physical traits were inborn and scarcely affected by the environment. Other students of eugenics developed the theme and showed statistically that no degenerate or feeble stock could "ever be converted into healthy and sound stock by the accumulated effects of education, good laws, and sanitary surroundings." Did that not demonstrate the importance of distinguishing among the races those which bred good and those which bred poor stock? Animal husbandry had long since learned that lesson. Was it not time to apply it to mankind, in the face of the pressing problems of contact and conflict presented by the Negroes, Indians, and immigrants in America, by differences in color in all the regions to which imperialism led Europeans? Gobineau had already demonstrated what might be the consequences of not doing so.

The application to the problems of the United States

was clear, for uncontrolled migration of strange races created an imminent threat. Dr. Nott pointed out that the white strain deteriorated with "every drop of black blood infiltrated into it." It was hopeless to imagine that an inferior breed could be improved. Inferior and superior races could not "live together on any other terms than that of master and slave." The thoughtless philanthropy of the post-Civil War amendments and of the unguarded gates of the nation had produced a crisis that demanded the most serious consideration of scholars.

The systems took form and became rigid. It was no longer a question of white, black, or yellow, of brachycephalic or dolicocephalic, of Aryan or Semite, of Nordic or Mediterranean. Such indications of color, language, and head shape entered into the computations, of course. But the objective now was a complete order of folk that would recognize the ways in which differences of inborn traits had influenced the various sectors of mankind. By the end of the century hardly a scientist questioned the necessity of doing so. These terms of reference had then been accepted even by such educated Negroes as W. E. B. Du Bois.

It would have taken a man of exceptional innocence to ask: what were they classifying? Whoever wished to read could see that readily enough. The books described, and even pictured, the racial traits of Laplanders and Berbers, Magyars and Japanese, Teutons and Hottentots, Anglo-Saxons and Slavs. In tables of impressive statistics, carried to two or more decimal places, could be found exact measurements of these peoples' social, physical, and cultural qualities. All that was clearly, definitely proved.

The question that was not asked was nonetheless significant. What were they classifying? Color? Nationality? Religion? Language? Why, in the United States, for instance, should Negro have been one category and Jew another and German still another? If color set one group apart, why did it not unite the rest? Or to put the same question in another form: how did the classifier know that in the case of the Negro it was color that was the distinguishing feature, in the case of the Jew religion, and the case of the German language?

The answer, never given because it was never sought, was that the classifier did not know. Sometimes there was an arbitrary quality to the choice among the multitude of available designations. Often the group was easier to define negatively than positively: the Anglo-Saxons in the United States, for instance, could best be described as a group with a common descent by excluding Negroes, Jews, Scots, Irish, and others. In truth, as the categories developed in refinement and complexity and were applied to a widening variety of social problems, the terms of scientific classification assimilated a variety of usages drawn from the store of popular stereotypes.

Americans, whether they were scientists or not, lived in a world of a variety of peoples. In the streets of New York, in the corridors of trains that rushed through the prairies, on the dirt roads of the rural South, the diverse types of a heterogeneous population learned to recognize one another by their physical appearance. The characters of serious literature, of the dime novels, of the comic magazines, of the vaudeville stage appeared as readily identifiable images—the bearded, hook-nosed Jewish peddler; the drunken, shiftless Irishman; the gaudy or ragged, lazy Negro; the stupid, soggy German; the avaricious Yankee; the tall blond Scandinavian; the hot-tempered emotional Italian; and the bedraggled poor-white mountaineer. These were caricatures of real men; and the function of the caricature here—and in other societies in which different people met—was to sort out the individuals in knowable groups.

The people who looked at Pat or Moe or Sambo or Hans did not see color or religion or ethnic origin alone. They saw an exaggerated complex of characteristics and they did not confuse the caricature with the real men and women they encountered in daily life. But the scientists made a system of the caricatures. Under cover of their elaborate terminology they used the identical stereotypes as headings for the entries of their tables. The attributes of the Jew or Negro or Yankee, isolated and classified, thus became genetic, racial traits—inbred and not to be shaken off by cultural or social change.

They had been trapped in a web of their own weaving.

For well over a century they had been committed to the assumption—which grew more rigid with time—that classification was the first step toward knowledge. If skulls and skin color could be classed in groups, who would doubt that men could be, and in the same way?

Long since, they had forgotten the warning of Buffon that "genera, orders, classes exist only in our imaginations. . . . There are only individuals. Nature does not arrange her works in bunches, nor living beings in genera." Rather, oblivious of the consequences, the scientists endowed the races they created with fixed, determinate characteristics, unaware that they were only putting an order to their own preconceptions.

In these decades of enormous achievement they had moved from the love of knowledge to the pride in it, and their pride would betray them. Events would soon reveal how treacherous their science could be. Meanwhile the science itself, in its application to a specific problem, is worthy of more intensive examination on its own terms as science.

CHAPTER V

Old Immigrants and New

BETWEEN 1917 and 1924 American immigration policy took a sharp and decisive turn. From the earliest days of the republic until the First World War the United States had deliberately permitted newcomers of whatever origin to enter freely through its gates. Unrestricted immigration had significantly furthered national development. Yet suddenly this long-standing tradition yielded to a new attitude which thereafter was so firmly fixed in the American consciousness that it has not yet been shaken off.

A combination of circumstances was responsible for the abrupt shift. The fears and distrust bred by the war and the unsuccessful peace nurtured suspicion of all that was foreign, of immigration as well as of the League of Nations. In addition some groups within the United States had come to consider their interests imperiled by the newcomers. The old Yankee families of New England, for instance, viewed with misgivings the rising percentage of foreign-born about them. The organized labor movement, made up predominantly of skilled workers, had become convinced that only a sharp limitation of the labor supply could protect its interests. In the first decade of the twentieth century substantial blocs of Southerners, former Populists and Progressives, each for its own reasons, came to regard the continuation of immigration as undesirable. The gradual accretion of strength in these groups contributed to the ultimate shift in policy.

Prior to 1910 there was no indication that all these dissatisfied groups would see the solution to their own problems in the restriction of immigration in the actual form restriction took. For the new policy aimed not simply to limit the total numbers of entrants; it intended also to select among them. The new policy drew a sharp distinction between the immigrants of northern and western Europe and those from southern and eastern Europe. In the minds of those who framed the laws of 1917–1924 that distinction was more important than restriction itself.

Basic to that distinction was a "scientific" assumption, one that subsequently proved false, but that was sincerely and conscientiously held in the early decades of this century. That assumption seemed for a time to have been validated and confirmed by the report of a governmental commission which devoted a great deal of time and energy to its investigation. Since vestiges of that assumption still influence our laws, it is imperative that we look closely at the commission which gave it authoritative expression. To do so will also clarify some of the problems of science as an instrument for directing government policy.

One fundamental premise lay behind the immigration legislation of 1917–1924 and animated also the McCarran-Walter Act of 1952. Embodied in the quota system, this premise held that the national origin of an immigrant was a reliable indication of his capacity for Americanization. It was averred, and science seemed to show, that some people, because of their racial or national constitution, were more capable of becoming Americans than others. Furthermore, it was argued that the "old immigrants," who came to the United States before 1880, were drawn from the superior stocks of northern and western Europe, while those who came after that date were drawn from the inferior breeds of southern and eastern Europe.

There was a demonstrable connection between the diffusion of this assumption and the course of immigration legislation in the first quarter of the century. Those who argued in favor of a restrictionist policy did so not merely, perhaps not primarily, because they wished to reduce the total volume of immigration, but, more important, because they wished to eliminate the "new" while perpetuating the "old" immigration. This was the logic of the literacy test. Writing in the midst of the battle for its enactment, one of its leading proponents, Prescott F. Hall, pointed out that the test furnished "an indirect method of excluding those who are undesirable, not merely because of their illiteracy, but for other reasons." After all, Hall noted, "the hereditary tendencies of the peoples illiterate abroad . . . cannot be overcome in a generation or two." And, looking back at the accomplished fact, the Commissioner General of Immigration pointed out in 1923 that the widespread popularity of the literacy test was "based quite largely upon a belief . . . that it would reduce the stream of new immigration . . . without seriously interfering with the coming of the older type."

The literacy law, passed over President Wilson's veto in 1917, did not, however, accomplish what had been expected of it. The end of the war brought a resumption of immigration and, with it, a renewed demand that the objective of keeping out the "new" while admitting the "old" immigrants be attained through the national-origin device. The result was passage of the Johnson Act of 1921. The intent of the act was clear. On the question of whether the base year should be 1910 or 1920, for instance, Representative Box pointed out that "the number of the older and better immigrants coming has been relatively much smaller during the last 10 years, and the number from southern Europe, Italy, and Russia much greater, which will be reflected in the 1920 census. The making of the 1910 census the basis will give us more of the better and less of the less desirable immigration than if it were based on the census of 1920." The act of 1924, which pushed the base quota year back to 1890 and consolidated the theory of national origins, was motivated by similar convictions as to the inferiority of the "new" immigrants. Congressman Vestal, arguing in favor of the measure, put the idea clearly: the southern and eastern immigrants of Europe, he said, "have not been of the kind that are readily assimilated or absorbed by our American life."

It thus becomes a matter of considerable importance to ascertain how the conception originated and gained currency that the peoples of southern and eastern Europe were inferior to those of northern and western Europe. At root this concept could be traced to the racist beliefs, freely expressed in the 1890's, that the peoples of the Mediterranean region were biologically different from those of northern and western Europe and that the difference sprang from an inferiority of blood and could be observed in certain social characteristics.

The argument was given forceful expression by the distinguished anthropologist of the American Museum of Natural History in an enormously popular book, one adjudged by *Science* a "work of solid merit." In *The Passing of the Great Race* (1916), Madison Grant adopted the line of Gobineau and insisted that the new immigrants were not "members of the Nordic race as were the earlier ones. . . . The new immigration contained a large and increasing number of the weak, the broken, and the mentally crippled of all races drawn from the lowest stratum of the Mediterranean basin and the Balkans, together with hordes of the wretched, submerged populations of the Polish ghettos. Our jails, insane asylums, and almshouses are filled with this human flotsam and the whole tone of American life, social, moral, and political, has been lowered and vulgarized by them."

These theories were bitterly and inconclusively debated through the early years of the twentieth century. The decisive turn in the argument came when they seemed to receive validation from the reports of two governmental investigations. The first was the detailed study by the Immigration Commission under the chairmanship of Senator Dillingham. The second was a report by Dr. Harry H. Laughlin of the Carnegie Institution, "the expert eugenics agent" of the House Committee on Immigration and Naturalization.

These reports had a direct impact upon subsequent legislation, for they supported theoretical opinions privately held with what appeared to be official and presumably scientific proof. The Immigration Commission, appointed in 1907, presented its conclusions in 1910 in an impressive forty-two-volume report. Widely quoted, the report figured prominently in the deliberations which produced the Johnson Act of 1921. Congressman Box thus took for granted that "the great immigration commission, which some years ago spent hundreds of thousands of dollars in investigation and study of this great question," had produced "conclusive reasons why we should encourage the coming in of the class which has been extolled so highly as an element which has contributed so much to our life and why it should discourage that which comes from Russia and southern Europe." In the same way the Laughlin report, presented in 1922 and printed in 1923, laid the groundwork for the legislation of 1924. This latter report was widely quoted in quasi-scientific articles and entered prominently into the debate as a result of which the act of 1924 was enacted. It therefore becomes a matter of prime importance to investigate the preparation of these reports and the soundness of their conclusions.

The Dillingham Commission was the outgrowth of a renewed attempt to enact a literacy test in 1906. The opponents of that measure hoped to block it, or at least to postpone immediate action, by calling for a commission to study the whole problem. Congressman Bartholdt, who proposed the creation of such a body, undoubtedly had in mind a congressional committee such as those which had already conducted similar investigations in 1891 and 1892. This was also the expectation of Speaker Cannon, who opposed any airing of the immigration question on the ground that it was an issue likely to divide the Republican party politically.

Although the question was one primarily for congressional action, it also deeply concerned President Theodore Roosevelt. In part he was moved by such considerations as influenced Speaker Cannon. In part he was also concerned because he was even then engaged in delicate diplomatic discussions with the Japanese. Ultimately these negotiations would lead to the controversial Gentlemen's Agreement to limit Japanese immigration by the voluntary action of the Tokyo government. At the moment Roosevelt feared that agitation of the general question of immigration might upset these negotiations. Finally, the President had great faith in the efficiency of fact-finding agencies as devices to evade the necessity for clear-cut political decisions.

Although Theodore Roosevelt accepted and supported the idea of such a commission, he subtly modified the conception of what it should be and do. He proposed to the Congress that the study be entrusted not to the usual congressional investigating committee, but rather to a number of experts, whom he would himself appoint. While the question was still being debated in Congress, he confidentially requested Commissioner of Labor Neill to proceed at once to "as full an investigation of the whole subject of immigration as the facilities at hand will permit."

As enacted on February 20, 1907, the law was a compromise between presidential and congressional wishes. It provided for an investigating commission of nine, three to be chosen by the President of the Senate, three by the Speaker of the House, and three experts by the President. In this form the proposal secured the acquiescence of all parties to the debate and also drew the support of a great number of social workers and social theorists attracted by the idea of an impartial, scientific investigation as an instrument of the social engineering of which there was then much talk.

At this stage, therefore, there was a widespread expectation that out of the deliberations of the commission would come a body of verified and indisputable facts which would supply the groundwork for future action. President Roosevelt summed up these expectations in a private message to Speaker Cannon when he expressed the hope that from the work of the commission would come the information that he could then use "to put before the Congress a plan which would amount to a definite solution of this immigration business."

The circumstances of its establishment account for the great hopes that were held out for the report of the commission and the prestige that was ultimately attached to its findings. That prestige was certainly added to when the commission took more than three years to investigate, spent a million dollars, employed a staff of about three hundred, and published its results in forty-two impressive volumes.

A view of the actual circumstances of the compilation and of the methods used shows, however, that the commission's report was neither impartial nor scientific, and that confidence in it was not altogether justified. No public hearings were held, no witnesses cross-examined by the members of the commission. Largely the study was conducted by experts who each compiled voluminous reports which were not printed until *after* the commission had reached its conclusions. It is doubtful whether the senators and congressmen on the commission ever had the time to examine the bulky reports in manuscript. It is most likely they were compelled rather to rest their judgment upon a two-volume summary prepared for them by a group of experts on the staff. The final report was "adopted within a half hour of the time when, under the law, it must be filed." The identity of the experts must therefore be of some significance.

The key individual was the economist Jeremiah W. Jenks. Jenks was chosen because he had served for a decade in a similar capacity on other fact-finding investigations set up to deal with trusts and other questions. He had already expressed himself on the subject of immigration; and, as a teacher, had long argued the necessity of restricting the number of newcomers along the lines the commission would later recommend. The other public members were Commissioner of Labor Neill and William R. Wheeler, active in Republican politics in San Francisco, which was then being shaken by the Japanese question. The crucial post of secretary was given, on the recommendation of Senator Henry Cabot Lodge, an outspoken restrictionist, to Morton E. Crane, described by the senator as "absolutely safe and loyal" on the immigration question. Roosevelt was perhaps less concerned with impartiality than with the likelihood of producing a tactically safe report. In any case, he warned Jenks, "Don't put in too many professors."

Despite its scientific pretensions, therefore, the report began by taking for granted the conclusions it aimed to prove—that the new immigration was essentially different from the old and less capable of being Americanized. This assumption is clearly stated at the very beginning of the report:

The old and the new immigration differ in many essentials. The former was . . . largely a movement of settlers . . . from the most progressive sections of Europe. . . . They entered practically every line of activity. . . . Many of them . . . became landowners. . . . They mingled freely with the native Americans and were quickly assimilated. On the other hand, the new immigration has been largely a movement of unskilled laboring men who have come . . . from the less progressive countries of Europe. . . . They have . . . congregated together in sections apart from native Americans and the older immigrants to such an extent that assimilation has been slow.

The assumption with which the commission started conditioned the preparation of the whole report and made it certain that the conclusions would confirm the prejudgment. To quote the commission's own words:

Consequently the Commission paid but little attention to the foreign-born element of the old immigrant class and directed its efforts almost entirely to . . . the newer immigrants.

The notion that the old immigration stood clearly apart from the new was directly reflected in the techniques through which the commission operated. There was no effort to give a time dimension to its data; there was some talk of including a history of immigration, but such a study was never prepared. There was therefore no opportunity to trace the development of various problems or to make comparisons between earlier and later conditions. For the same reason the commission made no use of any information except that gathered by its own staff at the moment. The enormous store of data in the successive state and federal censuses was hardly touched. For fifty years state bureaus of labor statistics had been gathering materials on the conditions of industrial labor; the commission disregarded those entirely. Instead it planned, but never finished, a mammoth census of all industrial workers. It overlooked similarly the wealth of information contained in almost a century of investigations by other governmental and private bodies.

Finally, the commission consistently omitted from its calculations and judgments the whole question of duration of settlement. Time and again it assumed that a group which had lived in the United States for five years could be treated on the same footing as one that had lived here for thirty-five. In a few cases there was enough information to make out the distortions that followed upon that premise. In most cases, however, the commission did not even possess the data on which a reasoned judgment could be based.

Taking for granted the difference between old and new immigrants, the commission found it unnecessary to prove that the difference existed. In most cases the individual reports—on industry, crime, nationality, and the like—did not contain the materials for a proper comparison of old and new. *But in the summary the commission followed the procedure of presenting the introduction and conclusion of each individual report, together with its own interpretive comments, which supplied the judgment on the inferiority of the new immigrants.* Those comments sprang from its own a priori assumption, not from any evidence—whatever that was worth; sometimes, indeed, they ran altogether against such evidence.

The substance of the report fell into a number of general categories. Volumes I and II were summary volumes. Volume III, a statistical survey of immigration, 1819–1910, and Volume XXXIX, an analysis of legal provisions, were noncontroversial. Volume XL was a study of immigration in other countries, with no bearing upon the general conclusions.

The critical material in the other volumes fell into nine general categories:

1. A Dictionary of Races. Volume V, summarized in Volume I, 209 ff.

2. Emigration Conditions in Europe. Volume IV, summarized in Volume I, 165 ff.
3. Economic Effects of Immigration. Volumes VI–XXVIII, summarized in Volume I, 285 ff.
4. Education and Literacy. Volumes XXIX–XXXIII, summarized in Volume II, 1 ff.
5. Charity and Immigration. Volumes XXXIV–XXXV, summarized in Volume II, 87 ff.
6. Immigration and Crime. Volume XXXVI, summarized in Volume II, 159 ff.
7. Immigration and Vice. Volume XXXVII, summarized in Volume II, 323 ff.
8. Immigration and Insanity. Volume II, 223 ff. Complete report.
9. Immigration and Bodily Form. Volume XXXVIII, summarized in Volume II, 501 ff.

It will be profitable to scrutinize each of these categories individually.

1. THE DICTIONARY OF RACES

In considering the monumental *Dictionary of Races* compiled by the commission it is necessary to take account of the views of race held by its expert, Dr. J. W. Jenks, and by the anthropologist, Daniel Folkmar, who was charged with the responsibility for preparing that section of the report. Neither man consciously accepted the notion that such people as Italians or Armenians were set apart by purely biological distinctions; such a notion could not have been applied to differentiate among the masses of immigrants. But both agreed that there were innate, ineradicable race distinctions that separated groups of men from one another, and they agreed also as to the general necessity of classifying these races to know which were fittest, most worthy of survival. The immediate problem was to ascertain "whether there may not be certain races that are inferior to other races . . . to discover some test to show whether some may be better fitted for American citizenship than others."

The introduction to the *Dictionary of Races* explained that while mankind may be divided into five divisions "upon physical or somatological grounds," the subdivision of these into particular races is made "largely upon a linguistic basis." According to the dictionary, this linguistic basis of classification was not only practical, in the sense that immigrant inspectors could readily determine the language spoken, but it also had "the sanction of law in immigration statistics and in the census of foreign countries."

Yet, in practice, the dictionary concerned itself with much more than a classification by language. Through it ran a persistent, though not a consistent, tendency to determine race by physical types, to differentiate the old from the new immigrants racially, and to indicate the superiority of the former to the latter.

a. *The biological sources of race.* Although the dictionary presumably rested upon a linguistic basis, it often considered biological inheritance the critical element in determining racial affiliation. The following examples will illustrate:

The Finns, it stated, linguistically belonged to the Finno-Tartaric race, along with the Hungarians, Turks, and Japanese. But the western Finns, who actually came to the United States, though they spoke the same language, were descended from "the blondest of Teutons, Swedes."

The Armenians linguistically "are more nearly related to the Aryans of Europe than to their Asiatic neighbors," but "are related physically to the Turks, although they exceed these . . . in the remarkable shortness and height of their heads. The flattening of the back of the head . . . can only be compared to the flattened occiput of the Malay."

Although "English has been the medium of intercourse for generations," the dictionary defined as Irish those descended from people whose "ancestral language was Irish."

Among the Japanese, who all spoke the same language, "the 'fine' type of the aristocracy, the Japanese ideal, as distinct from the 'coarse' type recognized by students of the Japanese to-day," was due to "an undoubted white strain." The "fine" type were the descendants of "the Ainos, the earliest inhabitants of Japan . . . one of the most truly Caucasian-like people in appearance."

b. *The differentiation of old and new immigrants.* All these racial identifications were confused by the evident desire of the commission to demonstrate that the old immigration was different in racial type from the new. Thus Jewish immigrants, though in language and physical characteristics akin to the Germans, were reckoned among the Slavs or eastern Europeans. In the same way it was suggested that a large part of the Irish were "English or Scotch in blood, Teutonic ('Nordic') in type rather than 'Celtic.'" The Dutch were the "Englishmen of the mainland."

c. *The inferiority of the new immigrants.* Throughout the dictionary and its summary were sprinkled reflections in scattered phrases and sentences upon the lesser capacity of the new immigrants to be Americanized. The English and the Irish came to the United States "imbued with sympathy for our ideals and our democratic institutions." The "Norse" make "ideal farmers and are often said to Americanize more rapidly than do the other peoples who have a new language to learn. . . . There is no need to speak of peculiarities in customs and the many important elements which determine the place of the German race in modern civilization." For "the German is too well known in America to necessitate further discussion." By contrast, the Serbo-Croatians had "savage manners," the South Italians "have not attained distinguished success as farmers" and are given to brigandry and poverty; and although "the Poles verge toward the 'northern' race of Europe," being lighter in color than the Russians, "they are more high-strung," in this respect resembling the Hungarians. "All these peoples of eastern and southern Europe, including the Greeks and the Italians . . . give character to the immigration of today, as contrasted with the northern Teutonic and Celtic stocks that characterized it up to the eighties. All are different in temperament and civilization from ourselves."

It need hardly be said there was no evidence in the report to support these characterizations. If the material in the dictionary proved anything, it proved that the people of Europe were so thoroughly intermixed, both physically and linguistically, that they could not be separated into distinct races. Nevertheless, the dictionary significantly established a pseudoscientific basis for the designation of various races. In the balance of the report the reservations and conditional statements in the dictionary dropped away, and the various immigrant groups were treated as fixed races, with well-defined characteristics. Furthermore, throughout, the commission proceeded on the assumption that these races could be combined into the two clear-cut categories, the old and new.

2. EMIGRATION CONDITIONS IN EUROPE

The commission studied the background of immigration by an extensive tour of Europe and through the examination of some of the relevant documents. It was interested in the causes of emigration, the surrounding conditions, the selective factors that operated in it, and the means by which the movement was effected.

In this section of its work, too, the commission deprived itself of the means of making appropriate comparisons between the old and the new immigrants, and then proceeded to make such comparisons to the disadvantage of the new immigrants, without the necessary evidence.

In approaching the subject the commission "was not unmindful of the fact that the widespread apprehension in the United States relative to immigration is chiefly due" to the shift in the source of immigration from the northwestern regions to the southeastern regions of Europe. It therefore "paid particular attention" to the latter group. Almost three hundred pages of the report dealt with the situation in Italy, Russia, Austria-Hungary, and Greece. These discussions were, on the whole, fair and factual. But they were preceded by a general survey of some hundred and thirty pages which drew less fair inferential comparisons between the emigration from these places and that from western Europe. The extensive account of the difficulties of life in the countries of the new emigration and the omission of any such account for the countries of the old emigration left the impression that the circumstances which caused the one differed from those which caused the other.

In the general survey the old and the new immigrations were said to differ on four main points—permanence of settlement, sex distribution, occupation, and the causes of emigration. In the summary (Volume I) these differences were stated even more strongly than in the more extended report in Volume IV. It will be worth examining each of these differences in turn.

a. *Permanent or transient emigration.* The matter of permanent or transient emigration was important because the commission presumed that those immigrants who came with the intention of staying made better citizens and residents than the "birds of passage" who came merely with the intention of working for a few years, then to depart. The commission stated flatly, "In the matter of stability or permanence of residence in the United States there is a very wide difference between European immigrants of the old and new classes." This conclusion it proved by comparing the number of arrivals in 1907 with the number of departures in 1908 as follows:

	IMMIGRANTS ADMITTED 1907	ALIENS DEPARTING 1908
Per Cent of Old Immigration ...	22.7	8.9
Per Cent of New Immigration ...	77.3	91.1
Total	100.	100.

If, however, the same data is taken for particular groups and presented in terms of the relationship of the number of departures to the number of arrivals, the case is by no means so clear. Such peoples as the south Italians and the Croatians would still show a high rate of departures; but, on the other hand, such "old" groups as the English, the Germans, and the Scandinavians would show higher rates of departure than such "new" groups as the Armenians, the Dalmatians, the Hebrews, and the Portuguese.

Taken even at its face value, this data would not justify a correlation between old immigration and permanence of settlement and between new immigration and transience of settlement. Indeed, the commission had available other kinds of data which pointed to the completely contrary conclusion. Most important of all, the discussion did not take account here of various conditioning factors, such as recency of migration. As an agent of the committee pointed out in another place:

It is true, no doubt, that most of the recent immigrants hope at first to return some day to their native land, but . . . with the passing years and the growth of inevitable ties, whether domestic, financial, or political, binding the immigrant to his new abode, these hopes decline and finally disappear.

b. *Sex distribution of immigrants.* The identical criticism applies to the commission's opinion that the new immigration contained a higher proportion of single men than did the old. Again, that judgment was superficially supported by throwing all the old and all the new immigrants together into two distinct groups; that is the basis of the commission's table:

PER CENT OF MALES AMONG IMMIGRANTS, 1899–1909

Old Immigration	58.5
New Immigration	73.0

But the specific groups of immigrants, taken individually, show no such clear-cut demarcation:

PER CENT OF MALES AMONG IMMIGRANTS, 1899–1909

Irish	47.2
Hebrew	56.7
Bohemian	56.9
French	58.6
Portuguese	59.0
German	59.4
Scandinavian	61.3
English	61.7
Scotch	63.6
Welsh	64.8

Dutch 65.5
Finnish 65.8
Syrian 68.2
Polish 69.2
Slovak 70.0

Here, too, the factor of recency of immigration affected the validity of the generalizations. But even taking the data as presented it is significant that such new groups as the Hebrews, the Bohemians, and the Portuguese stand better than such old ones as the Germans, Scandinavians, and English.

c. *Occupations.* The commission attempted to prove that the new immigration brought to the United States a significantly larger percentage of unskilled laborers than did the old. Its data did not show this. For the purposes of this discussion only, therefore, the Hebrews were defined as not part of the new immigration. That still, however, did not account for the large proportion of servants among the old immigrants. Furthermore, an examination of the specific immigrant groups once more reveals that the Germans and Scandinavians among the old immigrants boasted fewer skilled laborers than such new groups as the Armenians, Bohemians, Hebrews, and Spanish; and the Irish were lower in the list than the south Italians. There was certainly no basis here for the commission's distinction between old and new.

d. *The causes of emigration.* By confining the discussion of economic pressures on emigration to the countries of southern and eastern Europe the commission left the inference that the new immigration was more conditioned by such factors than the old. Thus the report stated, "a large proportion of the emigration from southern and eastern Europe may be traced directly to the inability of the peasantry to gain an adequate livelihood in agricultural pursuits." The statement could just as well have been applied to the peasantry of northern and western Europe.

Similarly the summary in the report asserted, "the fragmentary nature of available data relative to wages in many European countries makes a satisfactory comparison with wages in the United States impossible. It is well known, however, that even in England, Germany, France, and other countries of western Europe wages are below the United States standard, while in southern and eastern Europe the difference is very great." Actually the report itself made it clear in another place that the only evidence the commission had was on the disparity between wages in the United States and those in France, Germany, and Great Britain. It admitted that there was no data on southern and eastern Europe. Yet by assuming that wages in the latter places were necessarily lower than in the former, the data on the old immigration was made to prove the inferiority of the new.

3. ECONOMIC EFFECTS OF IMMIGRATION

This section of the subject absorbed the major portion of the commission's attention. Fully twenty (VI–XXV) of the forty-two volumes were devoted to it. The commission's agents accumulated an enormous store of data in all parts of the country; they examined twenty-one industries intensively, and sixteen others only slightly less so. Much of the material so gathered was, and remains, useful. But the conclusions drawn from it by the commission were often unsound and misleading, almost invariably so when it came to comparisons between the old and the new immigrants.

The commission began with the dubious assertion that:

the older immigrant labor supply was composed principally of persons who had had training and experience abroad in the industries which they entered after their arrival in the United States. . . . In the case of the more recent immigrations from southern and eastern Europe this condition of affairs has been reversed. Before coming to the United States the greater proportion were engaged in farming or unskilled labor and had no experience or training in manufacturing or mining.

By the commission's own figures this statement was untrue; less than twenty per cent of the old immigrants (1899–1909) were skilled laborers, and the percentage in earlier periods was probably smaller still. Starting with the misapprehension that there was a correlation between the old immigration and skilled labor and between the new and unskilled, the committee proceeded to draw from its material far-reaching conclusions as to the effects of the new immigration upon native and old-immigrant labor, unionization, industrial methods, new industries, unemployment and depressions, and agriculture.

a. *Effects of the new immigration upon native and old-immigrant labor.* The commission wished to demonstrate the adverse effects of the new immigration upon the existing labor supply. At one point it actually suggested that the new immigration diminished the volume of the old and reduced the native birth rate. But it did not push that suggestion far.

Instead it argued that in many industries the "new" immigrants *pushed out* the old labor force. It could not, however, explain this "racial displacement" by the mere willingness of newcomers to work at lower wages, for the commission discovered that in the case of the industries covered by its investigation it was not usual "for employers to engage recent immigrants at wages actually lower than those prevailing at the time of their employment." The line of argument took another course, therefore. The presence of the newcomers, it was said, produced unsafe working conditions and lowered the standards of labor to a degree that "the Americans and older immigrants have considered unsatisfactory." To have proved that would have called for a historical investigation of the industries concerned from which evidence might be drawn for the presumed deterioration of conditions. There was no such study and no such evidence. Indeed, this section seems to have been inserted into the summary arbitrarily, for it did not correspond with any section of the extended report itself.

On the other hand, the report did contain material, not used by the commission, that threw a different light upon the process of displacement. The investigators discovered that "the chief reason for the employment of immigrants" was "the impossibility of securing other labor to supply the demand caused by the expansion of the industry. Without the immigrant labor supply, the development of the cotton-goods industry to its present status in New England and other North Atlantic States could not have taken place." All these changes were part of the complex development of the American economy. The rapid industrial expansion of the half century before the investigation had been accompanied by a swift technological transformation which mechanized many aspects of production and thereby eliminated the skill of the old craftsmen. That accounted for the displacement. But the commission also found that those displaced, in large measure, moved upward to better-paying jobs made available by the rapid expansion of the economy. To the extent that immigrants contributed to that expansion they actually helped to lift the condition of the laborers they found already there.

In any case, no connection was established between the specific qualities of the new immigrants and the whole process of displacement. Indeed, the report itself pointed out that the shifts in the labor force went back to early in the nineteenth century and had once involved such old groups as the Irish. That might have suggested to the commission, but unfortunately did not, that what was involved was not some peculiarity of the immigrants from southern and eastern Europe, but rather a general factor characteristic of all immigrants, and varying with the recency of the group.

b. *Unionization.* The commission made the blanket accusation that "the extensive employment of southern and eastern European immigrants in manufacturing and mining has in many places resulted in the weakening of labor organizations or in their complete disruption." This statement was made without a shred of evidence. The commission did not include in its report any data on union membership, either for the country as a whole or for specific industries or specific unions. It had no way of knowing what the trend of union membership was, or what the relationship of immigration was to that trend.

The accusation quoted above derived not from evidence, but from the commission's assumption as to the nature of the new immigration:

The members of the larger number of races of recent entrance to the mines, mills, and factories as a rule have been tractable and easily managed. This quality seems to be a temperamental one acquired through present or past conditions of life in their native lands.

The lengths to which the commission was willing to go to maintain views of the effects of immigration on unions in accord with its prejudices emerge from a comparison of the account of the labor organizations in the cotton industry as it appeared in the extended report of the investigators with the same account "summarized" in the summary by the commission.

Speaking of the cotton-goods industry, the original report pointed out that unions were confined to the skilled branches of the trade while the immigrants were largely unskilled. The latter occupations "are not organized, and the coming of the foreigner there does not concern the textile unions." Since the organized branches of the trade were "protected, by the long time required to attain proficiency, from any sudden or immediate competition of unorganized foreigners, these unions are not strongly opposed to the immigrants gradually working into their trades." But "they manifest little interest in the immigrant employees until they have advanced to the occupations controlled by the labor organizations." Though the mass of laborers thus remained outside the union, the report continued, "all the operatives are strongly union in their sympathies and in the case of labor troubles have stood with the union people."

How was this summarized? Only an extended quotation will show the extent of the distortion:

The more recent immigrant employees from southern and eastern Europe and Asia, however, have been a constant menace to the labor organizations and have been directly

*and indirectly instrumental in weakening the unions and
threatening their disruption. . . . The recent immigrants
have also been reluctant to identify themselves with the
unions.*

This dictum inserted into the summary, in direct contradiction to the evidence, while the conclusions of the
original report were omitted, demonstrated the total un-
reliability of the commission's observations on the question of unionization and immigration.

c. *Industrial methods.* The commission's finding that an
increase in the number of accidents was one of the effects of
employing the new immigrants in industry has already been
mentioned above. In addition reference should be made
to the careful examination of the commission's conclusions
on the subject by Dr. I. A. Hourwich (*Immigration and
Labor* [2d. ed., N.Y., 1922], 458 ff.). Dr. Hourwich
showed that the commission merely accepted the mine
operators' point of view, which was to ascribe all accidents
to employee negligence rather than to deficiencies in equipment. Reconstructing the history of mine accidents, Dr.
Hourwich showed that their incidence varied with the out-
put of industry rather than with the character of the labor
force; and a comparison of mines in Oklahoma, Tennessee,
and Alabama, which employed very few immigrants, with
those of Pennsylvania, where the bulk of the miners were
immigrants, exposed clearly the falsity of the commission's
views. The commission, eager to reach its own final judgments, considered none of these types of evidence.

The conclusions of the commission also contained numerous miscellaneous statements as to the deterioration of
the conditions of labor and of wages as the results of immigration. In this connection it is necessary only to emphasize again the fact that the commission had no evidence
whatsoever to support these contentions. Such evidence
could have come only by a comparative historical study
which would actually trace the development of labor conditions over a substantial period. The commission made no
such study. The hypothetical and speculative nature of its
conclusions is evident in the following example:

Acknowledging that there was no evidence that immigrants actually worked at lower wages, the commission went on to say, "It is hardly open to doubt, however, that the availability of the large supply of recent immigrant labor prevented the increase in wages which otherwise would have resulted during recent years from the increased demand for labor."

d. *New industries.* The commission drew another unfavorable comparison between the old and the new immigration with regard to the capacity of the latter for stimulating economic innovation. The arrival of the newest comers, it argued, did not result "in the establishment of new industries of any importance." But, "by way of contrast, it will be recalled that a large proportion of the earlier immigrant laborers were originally induced to come to this country to contribute their skill and experience toward the establishment of new industries, such as mining and textile, glass, and iron and steel manufacturing." This assertion sprang from the unreal fantasy to which the commission clung, that the old immigration was largely made up of skilled artisans. It disregarded also the obvious difference between industrial conditions in the United States in 1840 and 1900. It was, indeed, easier to create new industries at the earlier date; but that reflected the undeveloped economy of the country rather than the quality of the immigration.

e. *Unemployment and depressions.* The conclusions of the report also contain a number of statements implying a relationship between the new immigration and unemployment and depressions. These are nowhere proved. In any case, as elsewhere, the commission found it unnecessary to show that the old immigration had stood in a different relationship; it took that for granted.

f. *Agriculture.* Here the discussion centered on a fairly sympathetic survey of many communities of recent immigrants. But the summary was preceded by an introduction, not particularly related to the report itself, which drew an invidious distinction between the old and the new immigrants with regard to the likelihood of their entry into agriculture. The comments disregarded two critical factors: first, that the number of farmers increased with the prolongation of a group's experience in the United States (this was revealed quite clearly in the commission's data, which showed that for all groups there was a greater percentage of farmers among the second than among the first generation); and second, that the American economy had changed after 1890. With industrialization there came a general growth of urban at the expense of rural population; even the sons of native farmers were being drawn to the city. Whatever difference existed between the old and the new immigrants was not the product of their inherent characteristics but of the conditions they had found and the length of time they had lived in the United States.

4. EDUCATION AND LITERACY

The agitation for the literacy test that occupied popular attention while the commission worked gave particular importance to its discussion of literacy and education, and to its attempt to establish a difference, in this regard, between the old and the new immigration.

The background was established in the account of emigration conditions in Europe, which clearly indicated a substantial difference in the rate of illiteracy. The original report examined the various reasons for the high rate of illiteracy in southern and eastern Europe and concluded, "But probably the most apparent cause of illiteracy in Europe, as elsewhere, is poverty. The economic status of a people has a very decided effect upon the literacy rate." It then went on to predict a steady improvement in the future. The commission's own investigators abroad thus recognized that the inability to read was a product of environmental rather than of racial deficiencies. The summary, however, omitted this optimistic discussion and instead made the sweeping suggestion that the high rate of illiteracy among the new immigrants was due to "inherent racial tendencies."

The commission also labored the point that the new immigrants in the United States were less literate than the old. The supporting documentation was nowhere brought systematically together; it was instead scattered through the reports on industries and agriculture. Criticism in detail is therefore difficult. But the general fallacy of the argument is evident enough.

The commission almost everywhere failed to take account of duration of settlement in arriving at the conclusion that "a much higher degree of illiteracy prevails among the immigrants of recent years from southern and eastern Europe than among those of old immigration from Great Britain and northern Europe." That is, in comparing the natives of Italy in the United States with the natives of Scotland, it calmly disregarded the fact that the former had lived in the country for a far shorter period than the latter. Yet that circumstance was of critical importance, as may be gathered from the data on the ability of employees in clothing manufacture to learn English, which does take account of it:

PERCENTAGE OF FOREIGN-BORN EMPLOYEES WHO
SPEAK ENGLISH BY YEARS IN THE UNITED STATES

YEARS IN THE UNITED STATES	PER CENT
Under 5	38.8
5 to 9	66.5
10 or over	83.0

The failure of the commission to reckon with the duration of settlement invalidated its whole comparison of old and new immigrants.

Its difficulties with the more general problems of education were even more obvious. The commission had apparently thought it would be possible to measure the capacity of the old and new immigrants to be schooled. Discussing the question, Jenks had pointed out, "Anyone who has observed, even in a small way, the different classes of people that come into this country knows that some are very much inclined toward making the best possible use of our schools, while others make no attempt whatever to get in touch with our educational system." The commission planned to make such measurements through an elaborate investigation of more than two million school children in order to discover which races were most likely to be retarded.

Although four volumes of tables came forth from this investigation, they proved nothing. To begin with, the data was defective since it was based upon questionnaires sent to teachers who did not understand them. "In a considerable proportion of cases," the commission acknowledged, "the teachers have assigned a 'cause of retardation' for pupils who are the normal age or even younger than the normal age for the grade." The commission nevertheless used the bulk of material gathered in its elaborate tables on "retardation," the very meaning of which many teachers did not understand.

The volumes of statistics that the commission reprinted thus reflect not the care and accuracy of the survey, but, rather, the fact that it was not able to shape its material to the conclusions at which it wished to arrive.

There was no basis in the data for dividing the old from the new immigrants on the performance of their children in schools. But the information in the tables did show a wide variation from place to place in the achievements of children within any given group. Thus 55 per cent of the German children in St. Louis were retarded, but only 21.2 per cent in Scranton; similarly the English showed 56.2 per cent in St. Louis, 19.1 per cent in Scranton, and 13.9 per cent in Worcester.

That might have suggested that the quality of schools and the social environment were more significant variables than parentage. But not to the commission.

Too, through the tables there ran a good deal of material that emphasized the importance of recency of settlement, so much so that the original report pointed out:

Length of residence in the United States has an important bearing on progress of pupils. It can hardly be expected that children of immigrants who have been in the United States only a few months or even years can make the same progress as children of those who have been here long enough to become more or less adjusted to their new surroundings.

But this reasonable comment did not seem worthy of inclusion in the summary.

5. CHARITY AND IMMIGRATION

The data on pauperism, dependence, and admissions to institutions did not provide the basis for any general comparisons between the old and new immigration, except insofar as the old were more subject to alcoholism than the new.

6. IMMIGRATION AND CRIME

"Statistics show," said the commission, "that the proportion of convictions for crimes according to the population is greater among the foreign-born than among the native-born." Furthermore, it concluded that "the proportion of the more serious crimes of homicide, blackmail, and robbery, as well as the least serious offences, is greater among the foreign-born." These statements followed smoothly from the conception of racial propensities defined in the *Dictionary of Races.* But to support them with statistical evidence was more difficult.

When the commission turned to the only existing body of information, the *United States Census Report on Prisoners,* it discovered a disconcerting situation. This data, gathered by a body which did not have to prove any conclusions, showed that "immigration has not increased the volume of crime to a distinguishable extent, if at all"; indeed, that the percentage of immigrants among prisoners had actually fallen between 1890 and 1904, and that native Americans "exhibited in general a tendency to commit more serious crimes than did the immigrant."

Obviously such statistics would not do. The commission proceeded to gather its own. For its study the commission accumulated a very large number of cases, fully 1,179,677, extracted from court records over a period of seven years. These were, however, derived from relatively few sources.

Of them some 1,130,000 were drawn from New York and Chicago, the two cities with the largest number of foreign-born in the United States, and 30,000 more came from Massachusetts, also a state of high immigrant density. (The remainder were the 12,000 aliens in federal institutions.) Apparently it was unnecessary to sample the experience of such places as New Orleans, Memphis, San Francisco, or Atlanta.

No inferences drawn from this partial data could possibly support the sweeping generalizations of the conclusions. Such a sampling would hardly be illuminating for the country as a whole, nor could it measure the pressure of the immigrant in the national crime problem. At most it might throw light on the peculiar problems of the two cities from which the bulk of the cases were taken.

The commission did not, however, use the source material as if it applied only to the communities from which it was drawn; if it had, its conclusions could not stand. Nor did it examine the frequency of crime relative to the number of the foreign-born and the natives. To attempt such a correlation, it felt, would not be feasible. Instead the commission organized the data to show how immigration had changed the character of crime in the United States. Its evidence, the commission imagined, proved that immigration had increased:

the commission of offenses of personal violence (such as abduction and kidnaping, assault, homicide, and rape) and of that large class of violations of the law known as offenses against public policy (which include disorderly conduct, drunkenness, vagrancy, the violation of corporate ordinances, and many offenses incident to city life) . . . [as well as] offenses against chastity, especially those connected with prostitution.

It must be emphasized again that at no point did the commission have the evidence to support its general conclusions that the immigrants committed a higher proportion of crimes than did the natives. Furthermore, it *did not* show that such a result had followed upon immigration. It had, indeed, no basis at all for comparison with earlier periods.

What it did was quite different. It traced the distribution of various types of crimes attributable to each group of immigrants and to the much larger group of native Americans. Within each group it compared the incidence of each specific type of crime with the total number of crimes in that group. That is, it reckoned up all the crimes charged to Italians and then computed what percentage of that number were homicides, larcenies, and the like. It did the same for every other group by nativity and then compared the resultant percentages for larceny or homicide. When, therefore, it said that the foreign-born were more prone than the natives to crimes of personal violence, it did not mean that the foreign-born committed *more such crimes* than the natives either absolutely or relative to their percentage in the total population. It meant only that such crimes accounted for a larger part of the total criminality of the group.

One illustration will suffice to show the meaning of this difference. The New York county and Supreme courts, in 1907 and 1908, showed the following cases of assault, by nativity:

COUNTRY OF BIRTH	NUMBER
United States	630
Italy	342
Russia	73
Austria-Hungary	62
Germany	47
Ireland	38
Canada	15
Poland	14
England	8

This data was presented by the commission in a table headed "Relative Frequency" of such offenses, as follows:

COUNTRY OF BIRTH	PER CENT OF TOTAL
Italy	28.9
Austria-Hungary	15.0
Poland	14.6

Ireland	13.7
Canada	12.1
Russia	11.3
Germany	9.1
United States	8.7
England	5.0

Only the wariest reader could avoid concluding from this tricky presentation that Italians committed more such crimes than the natives, whereas the exact opposite was true.

The table last cited could be accurately understood only if one remembered that "per cent of total" meant per cent of crimes of this category of the total number of crimes committed by the nativity group concerned. The high position of the Italians, for example, was not due to the fact that they perpetrated more assaults than the natives, but to the fact that they were responsible for fewer crimes of other types. In almost every instance the low rating of natives of the United States seemed due to the fact that the total number of crimes they committed was much larger than that of other groups. As the commission presented this data, it was never very meaningful, often misleading, and in no case supported the commission's general contentions.

7. IMMIGRATION AND VICE

The commission's finding on the "white slave traffic" was moderate in tone and factual in content. It was on the whole free of the conjectural elements that marred so much of the rest of the report. Perhaps the only objection to it was the failure adequately to place the problem in its context. Dealing exclusively with the immigrants, it gave the impression, unintentionally, that prostitution was largely a responsibility of the foreign-born, although fragmentary data in the report indicated that the immigrants were only a minor element in a more general American problem.

8. IMMIGRATION AND INSANITY

The commission did not make a firsthand investigation

of this subject. Its data was drawn from the census and other sources. While the available information seemed to indicate that the foreign-born supplied more than their share of the insane, it also indicated that it was the old, rather than the new, immigration that was chiefly responsible. The Irish, the Germans, and the Scandinavians showed the greatest relative responsibility, or, as the report put it:

It appears that insanity is relatively more prevalent among the foreign-born than among the native-born, and relatively more prevalent among certain immigrant races and nationalities than among others. In general the nationalities furthest advanced in civilization show, in the United States, a higher proportion of insane than do the more backward races.

9. CHANGES IN BODILY FORM AMONG THE DESCENDANTS OF IMMIGRANTS

The commission considered within the scope of its inquiry the whole problem of the physical characteristics of the immigrants. To the *Dictionary of Races*, which rested upon information gathered from other sources, it wished to join its own findings on the physical characteristics of immigrants and their descendants. This was an important question because it was theretofore assumed that such characteristics of a race as bodily form were fixed and permanent. It was not imagined that they would change in the course of immigration; and if they did not, that might conspicuously affect the assimilation of the immigrants.

Professor Franz Boas of Columbia University, the distinguished anthropologist charged with responsibility for the study, discovered surprising results, however. It appeared that:

the head form, which has always been considered one of the most stable and permanent characteristics of human races, undergoes far-reaching changes due to the transfer of the people from European to American soil. . . . This fact shows . . . that not even those characteristics of a race

*which have proved to be most permanent in their old home
remain the same under the new surroundings; and we are
compelled to conclude that when these features of the body
change, the whole bodily and mental make-up of the immigrants may change. . . . All the evidence is now in favor
of a great plasticity of human types.*

The commission was certainly surprised with these results. It perforce quoted them—but cautiously, and with
the reservation that a good deal more study was needed
before they could be accepted. The commission, however,
did not allow these findings to influence the materials in
the *Dictionary of Races* or to stand in the way of its allusion
to the fixed nature of the temperaments of the races it
discussed through the body of the report.

10. SUMMARY EVALUATION OF THE COMMISSION'S FINDINGS

In summary it may be said the commission did not use
the opportunity afforded it to make the open, objective
study of the problem it might have. It began with pre-
conceived ideas as to the difference between the old and
the new immigration. It did not find the evidence to sub-
stantiate that assumption. But it devoted much of its effort
to bending what evidence it could find to that end. Its
conclusions were largely invalidated by those distortions
and offered an unsound basis for the legislation that
followed.

Less than a decade after the submittal of the Dillingham
Commission's report the proponents of more restrictive
legislation sought further scientific support for their theories. They found it in the "Analysis of America's Modern
Melting Pot," by Dr. Harry Laughlin, a highly qualified
geneticist associated with the Eugenics Records Office. This
inquiry, commissioned by the government, was designed to
correct the inability of the earlier investigation to demonstrate conclusively the social inferiority of the new immigrants. Laughlin's report originated in a hearing of the
House Immigration Committee (April 16, 17, 1920),
which asked him to study the relationship of biology to im-

migration, particularly as that bore on the problems of social degeneracy.

Laughlin's analysis was presented to the committee in November 1922. Congressman Albert Johnson, chairman of the committee, examined the report and certified that "Dr. Laughlin's data and charts . . . are both biologically and statistically thorough, and apparently sound." Whatever the chairman's competence to pass upon these matters, he was satisfied that the investigation had proved the inferiority of the new immigrants.

The opinions that were before long to be reflected in legislation were summarized by Dr. Laughlin:

The outstanding conclusion is that, making all logical allowances for environmental conditions, which may be unfavorable to the immigrant, the recent immigrants as a whole, present a higher percentage of inborn socially inadequate qualities than do the older stocks.

This conclusion was accompanied by the assurance that it was based upon "data and conditions," and not on "sentiment or previous attitudes."

Before advancing to an examination of that data it will, however, be worth making note of Dr. Laughlin's own sentiments as he explicitly stated them to the committee:

We in this country have been so imbued with the idea of democracy, or the equality of all men, that we have left out of consideration the matter of blood or natural inborn hereditary mental and moral differences. No man who breeds pedigreed plants and animals can afford to neglect this thing.

Dr. Laughlin thus purported to be studying the "natural inborn hereditary" tendencies of the new immigrants to the significant social disorders. His method was to examine the distribution of various national stocks in 445 state and federal institutions in 1921.

This procedure was inherently defective, for commitments to public institutions did not actually measure the hereditary tendencies Dr. Laughlin presumed he was measuring. In the case of insanity, for instance, the standard of commitment was most inadequate, since the availability of facilities in various sections varied greatly, as did the willingness of certain social, economic, and ethnic groups to make use of those facilities in preference to private institutions or to home care. All the generalization based on such data must be dubious.

Furthermore, Laughlin's sample was faulty and he treated his material crudely, failing to make corrections for occupational, age, or sex distribution. His critical statistical device, "the quota fulfillment plan of analysis," was based upon a comparison of committal records of 1921 with the distribution of population in 1910, *although the census data of 1920 was available to him.* By this means he certainly magnified the relative number of the immigrants among the socially inadequate.

But all these methodological faults, grave as they are, shrink in importance when compared with a more basic criticism. *The data, faulty as it is, simply does not say what Laughlin says it says.* His conclusions can find support, of a sort, only by throwing together all forms of inadequacy in a few gross, and arbitrary, divisions, as follows:

	PER CENT OF QUOTA FULFILLMENT
Native white, native parentage	84.33
Native white, foreign parentage	109.40
Native white, mixed parentage	116.65
Northwestern Europe immigrants	130.42
Southeastern Europe immigrants	143.24

Laughlin's own materials do not support his conclusions if the various national groups are treated separately, whether for inadequacy as a whole or for particular types of inadequacy. In the chart which follows, the various nationalities are ranked according to their order in Laughlin's rating of quota fulfillment for each category and for the total. The ranking is in the order of descending desirability, that is, those at the top are most desirable, those at the bottom, least.*

* Not all Laughlin's entries are included, and Negroes are excluded, so that "native" refers to native white.

FEEBLEMINDEDNESS

1. Ireland
2. Switzerland
3. All Asia
4. Greece
5. France
6. Germany
7. Scandinavia
8. Austria-Hungary
9. Canada
10. Rumania
11. Italy
12. Great Britain
13. Turkey
14. Russia and Poland
15. Bulgaria
16. U.S., native parents
17. U.S., foreign parents
18. U.S., mixed parents
19. Australia
20. Serbia

INSANITY

1. Japan
2. Switzerland
3. U.S., native parents
4. Rumania
5. U.S., mixed parents
6. U.S., foreign parents
7. Canada
8. All Asia
9. Austria-Hungary
10. Great Britain
11. Italy
12. France
13. Greece
14. Germany
15. Scandinavia
16. Turkey
17. Russia and Poland
18. Bulgaria
19. Ireland
20. Serbia

CRIME

1. Switzerland
2. Ireland
3. Germany
4. Scandinavia
5. Great Britain
6. Canada
7. Austria-Hungary
8. U.S., native parents
9. U.S., foreign parents
10. U.S., mixed parents
11. France
12. Russia-Poland
13. Rumania
14. Japan
15. Italy

EPILEPSY

1. Scandinavia
2. France
3. Switzerland
4. All Asia
5. Greece
6. Austria-Hungary
7. Germany
8. Canada
9. Italy
10. U.S., native parents
11. Turkey (European)
12. Ireland
13. Russia-Poland
14. Rumania
15. Great Britain

16. Turkey
17. All Asia
18. Greece
19. Bulgaria
20. Serbia

16. U.S., foreign parents
17. U.S., mixed parents

TUBERCULOSIS

1. Switzerland
2. Germany
3. Austria-Hungary
4. Great Britain
5. U.S., native parents
6. Canada
7. U.S., mixed parents
8. U.S., foreign parents
9. Italy
10. Ireland
11. All Asia
12. Russia-Poland
13. Scandinavia
14. Greece

DEPENDENCY

1. Austria-Hungary
2. Italy
3. All Asia
4. Russia-Poland
5. Scandinavia
6. U.S., mixed parents
7. U.S., foreign parents
8. U.S., native parents
9. Switzerland
10. Germany
11. Greece
12. Canada
13. Great Britain
14. France
15. Turkey
16. Ireland

ALL TYPES OF SOCIAL INADEQUACY

1. Switzerland
2. Japan
3. U.S., native parents
4. Austria-Hungary
5. Canada
6. Rumania
7. Germany
8. U.S., foreign parents
9. Great Britain
10. U.S., mixed parents
11. Scandinavia

12. France
13. All Asia
14. Italy
15. Russia-Poland
16. Greece
17. Turkey
18. Ireland
19. Bulgaria
20. Serbia

A candid examination of these rankings will reveal that, whatever their intrinsic value, they did not show any consistent order of superiority or inferiority among the various nationality groups concerned. Furthermore, they certainly did not show that the new nationalities could, in any sense, conceivably have been said to rank below the old nationalities. All the inferences of the Laughlin report should therefore have been categorically rejected.

They were not. Instead they were widely accepted and significantly influenced American policy. The newspaper reader, like the member of Congress, took their results uncritically and without question. The one jarring note, struck by the Boas investigation into bodily forms, was quietly disregarded and not, for several decades, further pursued. Unfortunately the means of critical appraisal of these biased reports had long since been dulled by science itself, which had already led men to expect the results Dillingham and Laughlin found.

The studies that have here been examined have a historical interest insofar as they have contributed to the adoption of the national-origins quota system, which is still a part of American immigration legislation. By giving governmental and scientific validation to existing prejudices against the new immigrants, they helped to justify the discriminations against them in the laws of 1921 and 1924.

But these studies have also a larger significance: they show how vulnerable science was, at the beginning of the twentieth century, to penetration by images and conceptions charged with popular emotions. Those emotions sprang from a deep uneasiness in the hearts of disturbed men. To understand the hatreds and the fears that spilled over into the laboratories and that biased the computing machines, it will be necessary to look beyond the world of science at the human condition from which they sprang.

CHAPTER VI

The Horror

THE FALLACIES of nineteenth-century science ought never to cloud its real achievements. By the same token the nobility and dedication of the scientists ought not to obscure their human frailty. Beyond the impressive array of tables and charts, set apart by the elaborate formality of their procedures, were men groping for an explanation of their condition. No safeguard was adequate to detach them from the emotional impulses that also moved their parents and children, their relatives and friends, their servants and masters.

The inner disturbances that often pained all these people still survive in fragments of evidence. They cast oblique reflections onto the situations of contemporary literature; without the consciousness of the orator or author they speak out in the phrases of the sermon and essay; and they intrude, unrecognized, into the lines of the intimate letter writer.

Such scraps of data are not the material for science. They can neither be measured nor counted nor tabulated. Yet were some magic of imagination to shape them into a meaningful whole, then they might form an instrument for understanding the race hatreds that have divided modern society.

There are extreme cases, as when the usual restraints unexpectedly yield and the pent-up anger suddenly breaks forth and the men rush out and beat the victim to the earth.

These are lynchings and riots. They have occurred in Alabama and Detroit, in Germany, and Turkey, and Kenya, and South Africa.

At other times a colder anger evokes an iron policy. The offenders are to be bound down and set apart and made helpless, yes, and degraded so that the lurking danger of them shall be branded and limited and controlled. The etiquette of slavery, the laws of Jim Crow, of *apartheid*, of Nuremberg are the means.

Often, too, the anger remains within, a ceaseless irritant, assuaged now and then by the ability to slight or slur, by the satisfaction of holding the high places, by the recognition of superiority. It is a comfort of some value to have the inferior, in their low places, incapable of resenting slight or slur, known and identified, so one can be sure not to be counted among them.

Who were the victims?

They were Negroes and Indians, but also white men—Jews and Slavs and Italians—an indefinable host. For the victims were chosen to be such not by virtue of their distinctive characters, but out of the agonized need of their oppressors. Indeed, the actual qualities of Jews and Negroes before those people became the objects of prejudice were only slightly relevant to their persecution; the "non-Aryans" against whom Hitler acted and the Negroes who were segregated in the Deep South were not groups that could have been defined in any economic, cultural, religious, or physical terms that existed in advance of the onset of prejudice. Rather, those groupings were themselves the outcome of the prejudice situation.

It was not the difference, real or fancied, between the object and the subject of prejudice that was significant, but the condition of a whole society of which both were components, necessary to each other. Persecuted and persecutors were intimately alike in their condition as human beings. Isolated from each other in strange places, men could no longer recognize the brotherly gesture. Out of desperate uncertainty came a longing for alikeness, and then the dreadful consummation: to find oneness, the brothers divided, some through hatred against their Father's other sons, others through being hated. And not these or those made the hatred come, but the trouble that enveloped all.

That was the source of the dark emotions that, welling up, tainted science and justified the outrages of exploitation.

Once the men who had moved had set forth in tribes. They wandered across the steppe or edged out of the forests down to the plains with wives and children and cattle in the long columns of all their possessions. Home was where they were and movement did not disrupt the usual order of their ways.

It was quite otherwise in human experience when some among the Europeans of the sixteenth and seventeenth centuries migrated. Often it was a man alone, an individual, who went, one who in going left home, that is, cut himself apart from the associations and attachments that until then had given meaning to his life. Some inner restlessness or external compulsion sent such wanderers away solitary on a personal quest to which they gave various names, such as fortune or salvation.

They were a diverse group. There were priests who had brooded over the problem of a world in eternity and made the startling discovery that a holy mission summoned them away. There were noblemen in the great courts who stared out beyond the formal lines of the garden and saw the vision of new empires to be won. There were young men without places who depended on daring and their swords and were willing to soldier for their fortunes. There were clerks in the countinghouses, impatient of the endless rows of digits, who thought why should they not reach out for the wealth that set their masters high? There were journeymen without employment and servants without situations and peasants without land and many others whom war or pestilence displaced who dreamed in desperation of an alternative to home. Through the eighteenth century their numbers grew and, even more, through the nineteenth.

They had various destinations. The receding ships left them at the edge of an impenetrable wilderness; they

moved up the river and the dark jungle closed in behind
them; they came over the pass and the jagged forest shut
off the sight of the land they had left behind. They had
wandered indeed alone into the strangeness.

There was a preponderance of such men among the settlers of Virginia and Maryland; they gave a rowdy quality
to the colonies' early decades. A communicated restlessness
impelled their children's children over the mountains to
Kentucky and around through the valleys to the Carolinas
and Georgia. Later they would spread along the Gulf and
up the delta of the great river.

They were like other Europeans of the same and later
eras who came to the new worlds of America and Africa. To
them in their aloneness there was one pre-eminent danger,
the emptiness of the country about them. The world of
familiar objects in their place had disappeared; the wilderness remained. No church, no town or village, no judge!
Where was religion or law or morality?

There was only the dark forest, the secret home of unknown beings. What was fact and what was legend in the
minds of Europeans for whom the forest had been the forbidden place in a remote distance inhabited by the witches
and ogres of the fireside tales? They themselves were now
to be swallowed up in the darkness, to become themselves
beings of the woods. The awesome thought came to those
who were alone: no reckoning of right or wrong could find
them out here. They were helpless at the sight of the mys-
terious path or unknown growth, at the sound of the unfa-
miliar. Yet they had the power enjoyed by no king on his
throne: they could act without control. No authority could
find the secret out. That was the horror.

Some men yielded and, abandoning their heritage, became themselves creatures of the wilderness. Mostly, however, they refused to give way and insisted on living in
clearings in the dark. Within a circumscribed area at least
they made the effort to recapture the order that had gone
out of life at their departure. In the spaces in the forest
the old God could look down, the old church be re-estab-
lished, and the old forms of dress and behavior imitated—

if only they could keep out the wildness that ever threatened to break in upon them.

Beyond the outer circle of the clearing, among the strange beasts, were the strange men of the woods who recognized neither God nor law nor forms of behavior. Their presence was disruptive; often they were the enemy, to be resisted by every means, and it was then tempting to consider them inhuman imps of Satan. But then the enemy was not only without; he lurked by the corners of the clearing and sat by the shadow of the hearth. Was he the stranger whom chance wanderings brought to the same turning of the path, or one stranger yet by reason of the difference in language or color of the skin?

Or could it be that the enemy, more insidious still, was somehow deep within? Men who had lost contact with the norms of civilization could not avoid that fearful reflection. The untamed and lawless world about them was corrosive; under its influence all habits and ideas fell into disorder and the stabilizing line between the forbidden and the familiar lost the old clarity. Most of all, the Europeans under the strain of wilderness conditions feared themselves. Under pressure they had caught themselves in the nameless acts of cannibalism and bestiality. What other dark desires and secret impulses might not here emerge from within? Behind the necessity of always maintaining self-control was the ever present horror of the loss of it. That is why they were all extremists of a sort.

The line of settlement that flowed from Virginia was unique in the degree to which responsibility for control rested upon the individual. The attempt to re-create at Jamestown the social order of a commercial company quickly proved inadequate. The population dispersed into the interior and drifted westward for two centuries thereafter in individual fragments. The penetration of this Southern frontier was characteristically by the lonely man with his own possessions—beings and things.

By contrast the Northern settler shared the responsibility for control with a powerful social entity. The Puritan immigrants came to the New World in organized bands. They advanced onto their frontier, through New England and

New York and on westward, in orderly townships. They, too, confronted the perils of the wilderness; but their discipline was sustained, until well into the nineteenth century, by churches and schools and by the recognized prestige of their leaders.

The difference was displayed in the use of power against the creatures of the wilderness. The Europeans came with the intention of converting the Indian and of assimilating him into their own society. They were all to some degree disappointed. But the reaction of the New Englanders was limited and controlled. They permitted groups of red men to remain behind the lines of their advance in peaceful "praying" towns; and when they did strike out in fury against the hostile and independent, it was by the sanction and authority of the church and the state. The Southerner's encounter was more often individual. He was more likely than the children of the Puritans to fall in with the life of the Indians, even to take a squaw for himself. But he was also more likely to kill those who stood in his way, and with a savagery that matched their own. In either case the decision was one he made of his own accord, and that added to the strain of making it.

It was the same with the black stranger in their midst. The status of the slave in America was slowly defined in the latter half of the seventeenth century. But in the rural townships and the urban centers of the North the power of the master and the obligations of the bondsmen were limited and regulated by the community, which exercised a general oversight over all. In the isolated clearings of the South the law, half known and inchoate, was no restraint at all. The owners of the plantations, and of the growing numbers of Negroes thereon, could exercise over their chattels what harshness and kindness, what inclinations toward good and evil they willed. Again choice was a burden, and that heightened the difficulty of justifying the relationship.

The emotional tension of the Southern situation was agonizing in the Revolutionary period. In the North slavery could be abolished by the communal act of a legislature or constitutional body. Below the Mason-Dixon Line emancipation remained an individual measure, to be deliberated upon by men who believed in freedom and yet held others in servitude. Hence that longing for some magical ultimate solution that would cause the problem and its evidence to disappear. Hence also, after 1820, as the hope vanished of an ultimate end to slavery, the desperate groping after a justification, either in terms of the innate goodness of the institution or the innate separateness of those who were its victims.

By then, paradoxically, many of the conditions basic to the original disorder of American life had changed, although the disorder remained. In the first quarter of the nineteenth century the residents of the United States were preponderantly native-born. Europe was for them mostly a dim ancestral memory; they hardly missed the absence of standards they had never known; and the wilderness in which they had passed their lives was their home. Such men did not find the virgin forest or the empty plain hostile. Rather, nature here, untouched and uncorrupted, was almost divine; in any case, providentially set apart for the folk who would be nurtured by it. The thundering falls and lofty peaks, the very disposition of the continent, were evidence of the national destiny.

The altered view conformed to the northern assumption that all the residents of the nation would ultimately fuse into one people. The Indians, those children of nature, as James Fenimore Cooper described them, were conceded a nobility of spirit and grandeur of soul that would leave their mark upon the character of all Americans. The Negro, too, by his very suffering had acquired, like Uncle Tom, the dignity of Christian virtue.

Slaveholders, however, could not make that ready assumption. They could not forgo the assurance of the inferiority of the blacks that justified slavery. That inferiority could no longer be ascribed to the natural primitivism of the Negroes. It had therefore been necessary to ascribe it to some innate deficiency in their native character.

The compulsion to account for the degraded status of the Negro gave a special twist to Southern romanticism. Everywhere, in the cultures influenced from western Europe, a sentimental interest in the past was associated with emotional drives for individual self-fulfillment and self-expression. In the slaveholder that association took a peculiar, complex form. As a democrat he looked back to ancient Greece for the model of a glorious civilization that rested on bond labor; the Doric columns he attached to his house screened the Athenian orator from the realities of the slave quarters. Politics and the practice of law were the recognized modes of attaining individual distinction.

The planter's standards of personal behavior, however, were more likely to be drawn from another source. The plantation became a manor, the slaves were humble serfs, and he himself was the mounted knight, gentle in manners, gallant in warfare, respectful of the established church though not given to canting piety, chivalrous and honorable though capable of asserting his will through power, and disdainful of materialistic considerations. His highest obligation was to his own honor; and that honor was affixed to the woman who was his own true love. Surrounded by the voluminous skirts that were the symbols of her ladyhood, she occupied the center of his household. Chaste and virtuous, affectionate but not sensuous, hospitable toward her equals and kind but firm toward inferiors, the competent mistress but free of all manual tasks, she glided gracefully through the drawing rooms that were her—and his—domain, all as described in the novels of Sir Walter Scott.

It was a strain to live in accord with these images, the more so in the face of profound changes in the most intimate personal habits of men and women everywhere in the United States.

One unexpected source of difficulty was the rapid decline in the rate of mortality in the early nineteenth century. In earlier times the harshness and hazards of life and the absence of medical care made death familiar to every household. It was rare for a young bride and groom to live through the whole of their lives together, and widows and widowers entered upon second and third marriages as a matter of course. The partings of death were painful, but those who survived managed to accommodate themselves, with new partners, to the changing conditions of their age and status.

It was altogether different when life was prolonged to the point at which monogamy came to mean that the young man and the young woman joined in wedlock had to prepare to pass through all the stages of life together. Often unexpected discrepancies demanded subtle adjustments that one or the other could not make; and, while in time that would result in a rising divorce rate, for the moment it produced mostly unresolved tensions that embittered the relationship.

The fall in the death rate also disordered the place of children in the family. Offspring had once been part of the divine plan for procreation of the universe. The regular arrival of babies in the household had been a blessing, although one kept within limits by an unchecked, murderous rate of infant mortality. But as the mortality rate declined, parents, who were more often now spared the painful duty of burying their children, discovered they were left with another anxiety—how to provide for them.

Again the times had changed. On the expanding frontier farm the extra arms of a boy at the plow, of a girl in the kitchen, had been a welcome aid to the parent; and there was plenty of room for growing youth. It was different in the nineteenth century in the settled regions of the country. A father had to think of providing for his offspring and rarely could his own holdings furnish a livelihood for more than one family. It was not pleasant to think of the unwanted young men going off to the West or joining the army of clerks in the towns, or of the young women drifting into spinsterhood. In any case, it was a drain on family resources to give children a proper start in life. It was more difficult still on the plantation, for there a proper start called not only for land, but also for capital in slaves; and even the wealthiest parents had to consider soberly how many sons they could thus equip for life. Most difficult of all was the situation of the middle groups in the cities; their children required education and capital if they were to avoid a disastrous fall in status. Everywhere was a half-expressed desire to limit the number of births.

That accounted for the pervasive, if only partly revealed, curiosity through the middle decades of the century about the methods of birth control. The spectacular experiments of John Humphrey Noyes and Robert Dale Owen were but flamboyant instances of a widespread interest. It was a common calculation among physicians that the inventor of an effective mechanical device could earn "a princely fortune in a year." The columns of the press were crowded with advertisements of pills and potions; and the prevalence of abortion became a subject of concern to doctors and to social reformers. In 1864, despite the pressing concerns of the Civil War, the American Medical Association offered a prize for a tract "for circulation among females, for the purpose of enlightening them upon the criminality and physical evils of forced abortions." The demand for the printed little volume astonished booksellers.

None of the means then available was deemed desirable or feasible. The church, the state, and the medical profession united in condemning every artificial practice to limit the size of families. Birth control, like abortion, it was said, enfeebled the frame and produced a horrible train of disease. It was also a crime against nature and God, as well as against the state.

And against whom was the crime in the first instance committed but against woman? That rendered it particularly heinous, for she was no longer the daughter of Eve, the temptress who, for generations of Christians, had been the cause of man's downfall. A romantic glow suffused her character; pure in her spirituality, her capacity for ennobling man was all too often debased by his brute desires.

What conduct was natural and proper under these circumstances? The answer was hard to arrive at or, for that matter, even the form of the question. In this society it was not even clear who should be asked. Not the minister, or the parents, certainly; and the subworld of half information that passed from man to man was vague and unreliable.

Only the doctors who commanded the magic of science could speak with certainty. Frequently in the towns, and more often in the cities, from 1830 onward the lectures were announced "For Men [or Women] Only" and drew unabashed audiences of growing size. More popular still were the books which spoke in private and in confidence and told the honest truth. Their sales mounted to the hundreds of thousands.

The unanimity of attitudes in these works was striking. Man was endowed with the sexual urge in order to propagate the species. Unregulated, his desires would lead him by way of lust to ruin. Taking up with vile creatures or resorting to the "self-pollution" of masturbation, he might destroy his health, weaken himself, and ultimately pass his diseases on to his progeny. The phrenologists, who believed in a close correspondence between body and spirit, could trace the effects of unbounded "amativeness" in explicit detail.

But it took no special knowledge, in those days, to recognize the decrepitude and the physical deterioration brought on by sexual indulgence. A doctor in Utah noted the "marked physiological inferiority" of the Mormons. "Feebleness and emaciation" were common, "while the countenances of almost all" were "stamped with a mingled air of imbecility and brutal ferocity."

Providence, however, had created for man the "Divine Temple" of marriage, a kind of "sanitary measure" for his own redemption. For this relationship brought him into contact with a being "not naturally sensual like the other sex," one whose "yearnings" were "more mental than physical." Woman was "more virtuous and less passionate than man," whose coarse nature needed "to be polished and purified." If he in his blindness did not understand that she was "delicate and sensitive," constitutionally pure, and "finer wrought" and attempted to take at will "this hallowed repast of love, even though married by law," that was "that *forbidden fruit*, that *original sin*," which had once blasted men's hopes. The consequences were disastrous. "Carnality is carnality, the world over, in wedlock as much as out of it, and breeds contempt." Who yielded to such passions would languish in illness, shorten his own life, and breed corrupt and degraded offspring.

True love was of another, spiritual, order. It came to mature people, the men at the age of at least twenty-five, the women at twenty-one or more. Such marriages did not aim at gratification of the "animal propensities." But there were moments when the spiritual attachment suffused the bodies of the partners and, conscious of their obligations to posterity, they joined in blissful union for the purpose of begetting a progeny.

It was of the highest importance not to confuse that sanctified impulse with mere passion or all would be corrupted. Nor was it difficult to recognize the distinction, for nature had benevolently provided guideposts clear to all but the morally blind. In the first place the act was always to be in accord with its ultimate purpose, procreation. Therefore it was never to be consummated except for the purpose of producing children (and the proper intervals of childbirth, it was suggested, were at least three years). During pregnancy and lactation total abstinence was requisite; indeed, then the considerate husband would not even share his wife's room lest he use "up one half or more of the natural supply of oxygen, which God, in his Providence, had designed for her."

But even when directed toward a proper end, indulgence was not to be needlessly gratified; the lunar month suggested nature's own rule as to the maximum frequency of intercourse; "the generative powers would be much greater and better if the organs never had more than a monthly use." But man was safest of all if he allowed himself to be guided by woman's finer instincts and gave her the "rights of control in the sexual relation." The man who disregarded these laws, in harmony with science and revelation, courted destruction. Throwing "all his energies into an act which, for the time being, completely unnerves and prostrates him, and *accomplishes nothing*, without even a worthy purpose, he ought to feel ashamed; no wonder he seeks darkness and hides the deed."

Abstinence, repression, and self-restraint thus were the law; and violations were punished by the most hideous natural consequences, described in considerable graphic detail.

The readers of these volumes, the listeners at the lectures assumed the burden of a terrible obligation. They were the more literate, the wealthier, and the more responsible elements of society. They were already troubled by questions as to the proper relationships within the family —the number of children, the role of the wife, for example. Now they were overwhelmed by the guilt and shame the necessities of self-control imposed.

The burden was particularly severe in the plantation South. There the image of the ideal woman held a crucial place in the conception of social order. There the obligations of chivalry imposed particularly stringent requirements upon the associations of gentlemen with ladies. There, finally, communal instruments of social control were weakest.

And there were the Negroes, primitive ill-clothed beings natural in their behavior, the sight of whom aroused, or was said to arouse, sensuality. How often the helplessness or attractiveness of women who were their property led men and boys to gratify their will is irrelevant. The thought was certainly there. It lay behind the long line of speculation as to the consequences of mating different breeds; and it produced its triumphant apogee in the demonstration that nature made it physically easy for a white man to have intercourse with a black female, but impeded the union of Negro male and white woman.

More important, the act or even the thought of it was now infused with shame and guilt. In the eighteenth century slaveholders had been known to have colored mistresses, and to think little of it other than the necessity of providing for the offspring. By the middle of the nineteenth century, however, the connotations attached to the sexual act which might debase "the seed of Abraham" produced an intolerable emotional strain. What was the "natural instinct"? The master, drawn to the slave by her availability and repelled by consciousness of her inferiority, could purge himself of self-hatred only by locating the responsibility for the low passion in her, and in her not as an individual but as one of a degraded race of beings.

And the ladies in crinoline, for whom love was a tender, ethereal moment, with what pain they closed their thoughts to the fears of temptation that encompassed their husbands. And what slow, burning resentment they attached to the source of that temptation, and to the "mongrels" of every shade who were evidence of a yielding.

All that apart! There were plantation homes where perfect faith reigned, where a sense of honor and dignity kept men's actions and thoughts restrained. Still they lived under restraint and their judgments of the Negro were colored by the tension of it. Down by the quarters in the still night the blacks in their darkness gave themselves over to heedless abandon. They were unrestrained. No constricting reason held back the flow of their passion. That was the mark of the inferior animal nature that separated them as beings from the white. If a tinge of hidden envy entered into that affirmation, that only added to the emotional charge of the relationship. Prejudice now was more than a means of justifying exploitation, more than a body of ideas; it was a deeply felt need.

This was the extreme situation. In the half century after 1850 elements of it had appeared also among other groups and in other parts of the nation and produced similar responses of hatred and fear.

The Civil War destroyed the order of Southern society. Slavery died, and the plantation, and the chivalric ideal, except in pale dreams detached from reality; and new visions were slow to replace those which had been crushed in the battlefield. The situation of the Negro, now free, eased in the next twenty years. But the defeated whites could not extirpate the emotions of the past, nor would they surrender the justifications by which they had lost so much.

In the generation that matured during the last quarter of the century, and particularly in groups that had not been committed to the plantation, there were signs of fresh aspiration. Hope lay in a new South that would simulate the order of Northern family farms and industrial enterprises. The virtues of thrift and self-control, of hard work and careful planning would earn abundant material rewards. Such Southerners had thus assimilated an ideal of success that by the end of the century had an almost universal attractiveness everywhere in the middle sectors of American society.

There certainly were opportunities now for a rise in status. The expanding economy created a wealth of places in business and the professions, places that were rich in prestige and income. The clerks and small farmers of these decades could realistically aspire to see their sons owners of shops and managers in industry and doctors or lawyers.

But in a mobile society there was also constant danger of the loss of status. Everything was possible in a period in which the small rural town receded in importance, in which the village found itself ringed about with factories, and in which the family farm lost the stability it was never to recover. It was all very well to let the mind wander in the reveries of local-color literature about the bygone past. But no American could disregard the growing armies of the proletariat, of the hired laborers and tenant farmers, of the millions of tramps—all existing in the brutish misery that was the penalty of their failure. For the anxious father the risks of fall were as great as the opportunities for rise.

It was possible to minimize the risk and maximize the opportunity through a proper start in life; and now more than ever capital and education were the means. The young man who began with a stake to invest or with professional training enjoyed a manifest advantage over his competitors. His pluck and thrift and willingness to work would earn their full reward. Certainly it was incumbent upon the parent to limit the number of his children in accordance with his capacity to provide for them. Only thus could he be sure that his offspring would be among the fittest who would survive.

Science, too, by now had added confirmatory detail to what the young man and woman knew. Every reader of the popular press was acquainted with the ideas of evolution; and while few read the book, many had seen the title Darwin gave it, *The Descent of Man and Selection in Relation to Sex*. The proper conduct of married life was the determining element in the whole future of the race. The eugenicist added the weight of his opinion. Regard the achievements of the husbandman and the animal breeder, which depend upon careful selection and control! The private lectures and the published *Hints* spelled the moral out in the new terms. Choose wisely (with numerous illustrations of facial, cranial, and body types) and act with continence and purpose. When Weisman, toward the end of the century, proved the continuity of the germ plasm, that seemed the final demonstration that no subsequent environmental influence could undo the good or evil that stemmed from the marital relationship.

The importance of purity and control was then self-evident. What determined the quality of the stock? The answer was clear: selection of a proper mate and care in breeding. The wise man would be cautious in the choice of a wife and would not dissipate his energy except for the purpose of procreation. Abstinence was thus not only the sole available means for limiting the number of births; it also assured a breed fit for the struggle of life.

The wise course was not, however, easy to follow. Men who did not consider themselves weak found themselves inclined to stray under the tension of continuing restraint. The fault was not inherent in themselves. It came from without.

The presence of separate inferior races was a constant danger to the purity of blood. In the South the poor and middling whites had long shared some of the prejudices of the slaveholder. With Hinton Helper they had blamed the Negro for their own failure to rise. Now the blacks, free and equal in law, were also rivals and threatened, through amalgamation, to drag the whites down to their own level. Science added to the fear. Was the white man to take the place of "the gorilla," who, by the tales of travelers in Africa, "frequently steals negresses and carries them off for wives"? Nature provided its own punishment in the "moral obliquity and opacity of the human hybrid thus begotten." And behind nature stands God himself. "*He* has respect to 'race' and 'color' though the 15th Amendment to the Constitution of the United States has not, and He will send war, pestilence, and famine upon those nations who . . . fight against His decrees."

As the old abolitionist sentiment waned in other parts of

the country, the dread of color spread. There was an equal menace in the Orientals. Little girls were beguiled to "Chinese laundries under the influence of opium," wrote Samuel Gompers. "What other crimes were committed in those dark and fetid places" were "too horrible to imagine." What was more, science had revealed that skin color alone was no safe guide to race. White though they might be, the Latins and Slavs and Jews, unless kept apart, also might contaminate the strain.

All these inferior breeds were dangerous precisely because they were inferior. They were sensuous rather than spiritual by nature, and their women were "tyrannized by ignorant fathers and husbands." Their large families were evidence that they exercised no self-restraint, just as their poverty was evidence that they were being punished for their animal qualities. At best they were childlike and irresponsible; at worst their brute passions erupted in frightful outrages.

Poor Mary Phagan! Her tender youth blasted, her white body soiled, better that death should cover her shame. The stranger had done it. The fury of the men who stole him from the jail and left his mangled corpse dangling from the tree quickened in the horror of their own repressed emotions.

There was a more subtle danger also. Already in the 1860's some doctors had noted that while the birth rate of the better, white, native, Protestant families fell, that of the poorer, alien ones did not. The decades that followed confirmed that observation. The great cities, in particular, acted "anti-eugenically, sterilizing the best and leaving the worst to reproduce their like." In time, therefore, the growing number of inferior people would overwhelm the declining population of superior stock. After two hundred years a thousand Harvard men would have only fifty descendants while a thousand Rumanians would have bred fully one hundred thousand. "Extinction" was thus "the price of success." A relative handful of the able, thrifty, and hard-working would be left to support a great mass of degenerates, incapable of earning their own livelihood, charges on charity, and a corrupting influence in politics.

So civilizations declined, as Gobineau had shown. There was horror in the reflection that the low passions of the others would put to nought the painful denials that strained the lives of the virtuous. With horror went fear and hatred. But what action was appropriate was unclear.

The well-intentioned threw themselves into good works. The National Christian League for the Promotion of Purity, organized in 1885, grew rapidly in membership in the next thirty years. Its branches offered lectures on "spiritual and scientific mating," on "irreverent and foolish jesting with reference to marriage and courtship," on "varied aspects of race suicide," and on "teaching children self-control." Other folk agitated for laws to prevent the dissemination of information on birth control, for the sterilization of the unfit, and for the censorship of inflammatory literature. The women's-rights movement gained strength from those who believed that "social crime" was due to men who should be "punished with the utmost severity" and would be "when women share in lawmaking!"

By 1915 the results were pitifully inadequate. Nor was there lasting satisfaction in such escapes as the growing number of prostitutes offered to men or as the romantic tales of "maiden's virtue saved" offered women. A nagging discontent kept insinuating itself into the lives of families that would be ready for an orgy of hatred in the postwar years.

For a hundred years these passions had been stirred up by the inability of Americans to find personal order in the conditions set by their society. Although the attitude toward nature had changed, the disruptive effects of the wilderness persisted in new and more troubling forms. For in the face of the forest the original immigrants (and those who came later) had at least traditional forms to conserve. The native-born confronted their problem alone and unaided.

Huckleberry Finn, the story of an escape and a quest, stated the problem unambiguously.

At the start Huck was most "ready to cry." His society was going to rule him out, "because they said every boy must have a family or somebody to kill, or else it wouldn't be fair and square for the others." Then, all at once, he thought of a way, and offered them Miss Watson. "Everyone said: 'Oh, she'll do. That's all right. Huck can come in.' "

But life with Miss Watson was uncomfortable. Put into new clothes, Huck "couldn't do nothing but sweat and sweat, and feel all cramped up." Therefore he almost welcomed the kidnaping by his father, a man of the wilderness, compared to Adam. "It was kind of lazy and jolly, laying off comfortable all day, smoking and fishing." Soon he was unwilling to return. "It was pretty good times up in the woods there, take it all around."

Driven to flee by his father's violence, Huck had no intention of going back to Miss Watson. Rather, he joined company with the runaway Negro Jim, a man of nature nobler than his own father, one in whom were embodied Uncle Tom's Christian virtues—forbearance, humility, faith, and kindness. Once united, the man and the boy set off on a long drifting journey down the river.

Both are escaping. But both are also seeking something. Only Jim knows his own intentions. He is in flight to avoid being sold to New Orleans and thus forever separated from his wife and children. He seeks freedom to be back with his family; "he cared as much for his people as white folks does for their'n." Huck, on the other hand, knows no more than that he is lacking and incomplete.

On the way down Huck slips in and out of a succession of families. There is no place for him. At last, taken for Tom Sawyer, he finds a home for a while with his friend's relatives. They were joyful. But "it warn't nothing to what I was; for it was like being born again, I was so glad to find out who I was." There is security in belonging and satisfaction in knowing one's own identity. But Huck remains ambivalent. When finally he faces the prospect of returning to live with Aunt Sally as a genuine member of the Sawyer family, he balks. "I reckon I got to light out for the Territory ahead of the rest, because Aunt Sally she's going to adopt me and sivilise me, and I can't stand it. I been there before."

They had all been there before.

Americans of the nineteenth century were torn. The image of the "true family," one "established and conducted on the Divine basis," was clear. Loyal husband, virtuous wife, and obedient children, all "are to do all they can for one another" to "seek each other's holiness, usefulness and happiness." Each "esteems the others better than himself." What never-failing comfort and security was in this truly Christian order!

Only, so often, people felt "all cramped" in the family which seemed everlastingly to hold the individual in with its sticky restraints. It was well enough to dedicate oneself to the others, and to posterity, but when and where did the *I* come in? Americans were ever in rebellion against that which they cherished.

Constant mobility heightened the ambivalence of these emotions. So long as the brood was intact, the constraints of closeness in the nest were most irritating. Only when the man or woman, cut loose, set out for the West or the city did he miss the warmth and security of having belonged. Then descended the overwhelming longing for what had been left behind, the longing which from Jamestown westward had been the melancholy accompaniment of American settlement.

The ties, once severed, could never be replaced. The lonely man gazing out into the darkness of the forest or upon the empty prairies or down the endless corridors of the city streets saw never a monument of his belonging. Detached from his past, he could hardly be sure of his own identity. And as he regarded that posterity for which he was ever making some sacrifice, he knew in his heart that his children would desert him as he had deserted his parents. That was the horror. All the emotions once safely embedded by tradition and communal custom in the family had now no stable foundation in reality.

Hence the avid wish for some more comprehensive entity into which these emotions could be subsumed. All those pathetic fantasies of the nineteenth century, whether located in the past or the future, were dreams in which men attached to communities or races the loyalty, the sense of identification and communion they could no longer attach with safety to the family.

Alas, they were only fantasies. How could a race come actually to exist?

Yet with mounting intensity men willed that it should. It was an inmost necessity of their being that they should come to recognize their brothers. If they could exclude or set apart the strangers, the outsiders, then they might somehow come to know each other. It was as if only by creating an antagonist upon whom all the hatred and fear within them could be expended could they find a communion of the unexcluded that would summon up their capacities and longings for love.

This was America. But America in the uniqueness of its extreme situation often foreshadowed the destiny of the whole Western world of Europe.

The men who went out to settle the Spanish and Portuguese colonies of the New World and those who manned the British and French stations in Asia were unlike the Americans in at least one essential respect: they found not the wilderness, but going societies of considerable stability upon which they could graft their own institutions. In addition some, like the French in Canada or the Spaniards in Mexico, brought with them a hierarchical church that suffused their lives with traditional authority. In either case their problem was to establish an etiquette of relationships between conquered and conquerors; and often, as in India, they could build upon indigenous caste systems in doing so.

Not until late in the nineteenth century, with the development of imperialism in nations that considered themselves free, was there a compulsion to justify exploitation in terms of the inherent inferiority of the exploited. Then the racist ideas sprang into significance, particularly with regard to Africa, which most closely approached the conditions of the American wilderness.

Even so there was a difference. The Britishers in India or the *colons* in Algeria had not cut themselves apart from England or France to the same degree as had the Virginians. In most of Africa and Asia the return remained possible and desirable, as it was not in America. In this respect perhaps only South Africa was similar.

The full sense of alienation and homelessness appeared, outside of the United States, in the great new cities of central Europe. In Vienna, Munich, Berlin, Warsaw a massive heterogeneous population accumulated rapidly. Unprovided for and cut off from tradition, the proletariat, and the lower elements of the middle class who were in danger of sinking into the proletariat, felt also the disorganizing strains of unsettled family life. They, too, were moved by fear of the annihilated personality; and they, too, recoiling in horror, sought an antagonist to hate in order to discover their own identity.

It was their horror, and ours, that in doing so they found at hand the available instrument of the totalitarian state, which clothed them in uniforms, set them marching in ranks, and gave unexpected dimensions to their prejudice.

Recovery

CHAPTER VII

American Minorities Today

THE END of the world war in 1918 brought no peace to the United States. The Huns, the visible enemy, had been defeated. But the fruits of victory vanished before they could be tasted.

The momentary elation of common effort in the struggle faded away and, returning to normalcy, Americans discovered that certain problems of the past were still with them. A brief depression soon stirred qualms about the economy that even the subsequent boom did not abate. The color question was alive as ever; indeed, by virtue of the migration of the Negroes, it had spread to the North. The flow of new immigrants resumed. And the inner tensions of the whole society were no less painful than before. Prohibition and crime, jazz and a generation without standards, the decline of morality and the rise of the divorce rate were evidence.

Despite the platitudes of the optimists the prospects for healthy social recovery were not bright. Ominously the term "minority" came into more frequent use as a description of various groups in the United States. The word had been borrowed from Europe, where it referred to such people as the Ukrainians in Poland or the Germans in Czechoslovakia. Discussion of the terms of the peace treaties had made it familiar to Americans. In the transfer to the New World context, however, it acquired a significantly different connotation.

In Czechoslovakia or Poland it had been assumed that the preponderant majority of the population shared common traits of national origin, and, standing apart from the homogeneous majority of Czechs or Poles, there remained minority clumps of Germans or Ukrainians. The same meaning did not hold across the Atlantic. In the United States there was no majority in that sense; all the groups which considered themselves minorities after 1918, added together, were more than a majority of the total population. Furthermore, such people as the Catholics, the Germans, or the Negroes, who applied the term to themselves, by no means acknowledged thereby that they were less American in nationality than anyone else.

Minority, therefore, was not given a quantitative meaning; it had no reference to a consciousness of greater or lesser size. Rather, it reflected an awareness on the part of some groups in the United States that they were underprivileged in access to the opportunities of American life. These were folk who suffered from social or political or economic discrimination by virtue of their identification as inferiors or outsiders.

Discrimination was the permanent manifestation of the hostilities bred by racism. It had long since limited the rights of the Negro and, with the development of racist ideas and emotions, had, by 1918, come to apply with increasing frequency to other groups as well. In the decade after the end of the war it seriously abridged the privileges of men distinguishable by their color, like the Negroes and Japanese, by their religion, like the Jews and Catholics, and by their national origins, like the Italians and Poles. Discrimination then was supported by a well-developed code of practices, by the active agitation of political movements, and by an ideology that justified the separateness and the inferiority of the underprivileged. That complex survived until the middle of the 1930's; its collapse has created the situation in which the minorities now find themselves.

By 1918 a tightly meshed pattern of discriminatory practices put substantial portions of the American population at an enormous disadvantage in almost every aspect of life.

The inferiority of which such people were often accused was well on the way to being forced upon them.

Of the groups marked off by color the Negroes were most important, by virtue of their numbers, of their long history in the country, and of the tragic injustices to which they had already long been subject. Their progress since slavery had been painfully slow. Emancipation after the Civil War had stricken from them the shackles of legal bondage, but it had not succeeded in endowing them with rights equal to those of other citizens. Once the interlude of Reconstruction had passed, the white South, redeemed, had developed a way of life that maintained and extended the actual inferiority of the blacks. In the last decade of the nineteenth century one device after another had deprived them of the ballot and of political power; their own lack of skill and of capital, as well as discrimination, had confined them to a submerged place in the economy; and the rigid etiquette of segregation made their social inferiority ever clearer. In no aspect of his life could the Negro escape awareness that he was decisively below the white, hopelessly incapable of rising to the same opportunities as his former masters. If ever he lost sight of that fact central to his existence, the ever present threat of lynching and other forms of violence reminded him of it.

Progress in ameliorating their condition down to 1917 had been too slow to kindle the flame of hope among the Negroes, and the momentary flare of enthusiasm during the war quickly subsided. Thereafter there were few sober reasons for optimism. A slowly developing middle class offered the hope of personal improvement to a tiny handful. A gradual movement to the Northern cities offered an escape from the South but not an escape from the problems of discrimination; poverty, violence, and disorder dogged their heels in Chicago and Harlem as they had in Alabama or Georgia. The limited degrees of improvement were minuscule in comparison with the way that still remained to go. And when the depression struck in the 1930's, the Negroes, who were first to suffer in both the North and the South, faced a future of desperate futility.

No other group suffered the total burden of discrimina-

tion the Negro bore. Yet the Japanese and the Indians, also
set off by their color, had their share of grievances. For
them also the postwar period brought no confidence that
a remedy was within sight.

It was the same with some groups made distinctive by
religious affiliation. Catholics were widely reproached for
being un-American. The hostile sentiments stirred up by
the American Protective Association (the A.P.A. in the
1890's had never died down, and during the war there had
been ugly rumors that the Pope was somehow favoring the
Central Powers. Was it possible that he intended ultimately to subvert American democracy? The suspicion
ebbed and flowed, but never altogether receded; and sto-
ries remained current of arms stored in churches, of mys-
terious international emissaries, and of strange doings in
convents and monasteries.

Catholicism was also a burden to its communicants. The
presidential campaigns of 1924 and 1928, the savage hatreds that led numerous Democrats to desert their party
left many Catholics with the conviction that their faith
was a distinct political liability. Nor were they likely to find
reassurance in the efforts to outlaw parochial schools and
otherwise to limit the rights of their coreligionists. In their
day-to-day existence, too, boycotts of their businesses, discrimination in employment, and exclusion from important
areas of social life embittered their relationships with other
Americans.

The forces that generated the attacks against Catholics
found another target in the Jews. From the 1880's onward
a developing pattern of slights and formal barriers closed
clubs and restaurants and hotels to these people and narrowed the range of their social contacts. Early in the
twentieth century they began to feel the effects of discrimination in employment and of restriction in housing. After
the end of the First World War they discovered also that
their access to many educational institutions and to some
of the professions, like medicine and engineering, was being limited.

By then, moreover, they were the victims of the full bar-
rage of anti-Semitic accusations. The old stereotype of the
Jew acquired a sinister connotation. He was the interna-

tional banker, but also the inflamed radical responsible for communist revolution in eastern Europe. Above all, he was the agent of a vast conspiracy designed to enslave America. Henry Ford's *International Jew* and the pages of his Dearborn *Independent* exposed the plot of the elders of Zion to conquer the whole world. Repercussions of the credulous acceptance of these charges poisoned the relationships of Jews with their neighbors throughout the decade.

The enemy now took the form of groups set off by their differences of national origin. In the twenty years before the First World War millions of newcomers had arrived in the United States from parts of Europe and Asia which had not theretofore produced a heavy volume of immigration. The host of aliens from Italy, from Poland, from Greece, and from Austria, disembarking in massive numbers within a very short period, evoked a reaction of shock and hostility from some Americans longer settled. All the findings of science cast doubt upon the capacity of these strange, outlandish people to adjust to the ways of American life. Totally unassimilable, they were bound to lower all national values. Beaten men from beaten stocks, they should not be entrusted with the equal rights they would, in any case, never be able to enjoy.

Possession of a Slavic or Italian name became a decisive liability. A widespread, if informal, network of discriminatory practices limited the opportunities of these people and gave subtle expression to a hostility that occasionally, as in West Frankfort, Illinois, in 1920, erupted in passionate violence.

The discriminatory practices against the minorities were supported and extended by organized movements of considerable strength aimed to make them more rigid and more consistent. The anti-Catholic A.P.A. had passed from the scene at the opening of the century. But its burden was taken up, in the South, by the followers of Tom Watson and carried by a variety of smaller groups down to the outbreak of the war. There was an interval of relaxation during the war itself while all such energies and tensions were subsumed in the more general emotions of the struggle against Germany.

Peace, however, brought a return to the effort to organize race hatred, now in the form of the new Ku Klux Klan. Founded in Georgia in 1915, in imitation of the Reconstruction Klan but without any clear definition of purpose, the society grew very slowly in the next five years. Then suddenly its membership rolls expanded with an explosive rapidity that astounded even its promoters. By 1924, no longer purely Southern, it may have had more than four million in its ranks, certainly not less than three. By then also it exerted a substantial influence in politics.

The hooded men who solemnly gave themselves absurd titles and paraded in their ghostly costumes were animated by the fear of the Catholic, the Jew, and the Negro. But in their own pathetic, if dangerous, way they were also trying to restore a kind of order and morality that had all but disappeared from American life. Their own preconceptions had left them no way of seeking decency other than in the indecencies of the whipping, the burning cross, and the boycott.

The Klan died. The revelation of the crookedness of its leaders and internal dissension drove away the mass of well-intentioned who had joined in good faith. But the spirit of the Klan lived on through the 1930's. Under the impact of the depression hundreds of proto-fascist movements sprang into being and attracted into their ranks even more diverse groups than had the Klan. The crisis of economic collapse and unemployment, stretching onward without apparent hope of end and desperately unsettling millions of men, created a mass frightened and angry, and ready to be recruited by the Silver Shirts, the Christian Front, and a host of similar societies. Hatred held these people together, for there seemed no available means for social reconstruction other than limitation of the rights of the outsiders—however defined.

The marching men and the practices of discrimination drew sustenance from the ideology of race through the postwar decade. The Negroes and the Jews and the Italians were different from the original Americans, and their inferiority justified the difference in rights accorded to them. That justification rested on the solid foundation of the theory of inherent racial differences which divided the various species of mankind from one another. The conception now had the solid support of geneticists like Lathrop Stoddard and Harry Laughlin, of anthropologists like Henry Fairfield Osborn and Madison Grant, of social scientists like Henry Pratt Fairchild, Ellsworth Huntington, and John R. Commons. It was used to rewrite parts of the history of the United States; it served widely read journalists as a matter of course; and it became a consequential element in literary criticism. "The determinism of racial heritage" was in 1928 "a factor which all intelligent students of comparative politics take into their reckoning." Meanwhile psychologists like Robert M. Yerkes, Carl C. Brigham, and William McDougall had used the Army intelligence tests to investigate the innate qualities of the American stocks. The conclusion was that "the intellectual superiority of our Nordic group over the Alpine, Mediterranean and Negro groups has been demonstrated." Significantly, *The Passing of the Great Race* in a new edition sold more widely than ever before.

Yet this tightly intermeshed body of ideas, practices, and movements was shortly to vanish. Somewhere, in the mid-1930's, there was a turn. Americans ceased to believe in race, the hate movements began to disintegrate, and discrimination increasingly took on the aspect of an anachronistic survival from the past rather than a pattern valid for the future. The result was the profound social revolution that has quietly been transforming some aspects of American society in the past twenty years.

The collapse of the theory was most dramatic. A few older scholars who lingered on into the next decade retained the attachment to the older ideas, largely out of a sense of commitment. But even they were not likely to express their views in the open tones of the 1920's. And newer developments in genetics and anthropology, in sociology and the other social sciences quickly discredited racism. By 1940 it was difficult to find a serious, reputable American exponent of the racist views once so widely held.

Nor did the racist organizations fare better. They seem to have reached their peak in membership in 1936 and

1937. Thereafter they fell into a noticeable decline. Even
their effort to enlist isolationist support between 1939 and
1941 did not stay the falling off in the number of their
members. And the war put an end to their influence. Some
of them had been linked to the German and Italian governments; others had earned a reputation for disloyalty. The
unlovely spectacle of their leaders on trial for sedition dis-
couraged all but their most hardened followers.

Furthermore, peace after 1945 did not restore their
strength. True, some of the old chiefs, heartened by the
recollection of an earlier postwar period, took up the old
stands. But they found no converts. Even now a handful
wander through the hinterland repeating the stale warnings
of doom and competing with itinerant revivalists and faith
healers for dwindling audiences. They evoke no response.
They have been unable to capitalize upon the security question, upon the communist atom spies, or even upon the
fears of desegregation—issues that would have been god-
sends to their predecessors two decades ago. Nowhere do
they constitute a serious factor in American society.

Most important of all, discriminatory practices have substantially abated in these years. The United States has by
no means realized the utopia of total equality. Evidence of
discrimination still forms blemishes upon its life. But the
pattern has been irreparably shattered. The degree of improvement since the war has far outdistanced the most
optimistic expectations even of those who led the fight for
equality in the 1930's.

The Negroes offer the most instructive example. North
and South, they still suffer from injustices and still have
legitimate grievances. But the integrity of the patterns of
segregation has decisively been broken, and it is a matter of
time before equality of status and opportunity is within
reach.

During the war race riots in New York, Detroit, and Los
Angeles seemed an evil omen of what might follow. But
the danger did not materialize. Occasional sporadic out-
bursts of violence grow ever less frequent and lynching has
almost totally disappeared. An individual tragedy could still
strike down Emmett Till. But the sense of shame with

which that outrage was greeted, everywhere but in Mississippi, shows that the Negroes as a group, North and South, no longer labor under the constant fear of violent reprisal.

Steadily colored Americans have also been gathering political force. In 1940 they were already a substantial bloc in Northern cities, and the increase of their numbers there has led to a corresponding increase in their political influence. More significant for the future, they have also begun to make their voices felt within the South. The decision of the United States Supreme Court in the *Classic* case in 1941 destroyed the stronghold of the white primary, which until then had excluded them from the only effective election in the region. With the failure of successive subterfuges to circumvent that decision, growing numbers of whites have come to accept the fact that the Negro has a legitimate place at the polls. The number of black voters has risen consistently; they can no longer be disregarded as a factor in the political situation in Texas, in North Carolina, or even in Alabama. North and South, some among them have moved into important offices, and now supply leadership to the others.

So, too, many economic barriers that once impeded the career of the Negro have been leveled. The manpower crisis during the war began a continuing process of expansion in opportunities. In some states fair employment acts specifically forbid discrimination on account of color. But even where no such acts exist, Negroes have moved steadily, and with relatively light friction, into skilled, clerical, and managerial jobs and into the professions. The trade unions, once an important source of resistance, have, for the most part, arrived at a larger view of their own interests, which enables them to understand that discrimination weakens all labor.

There are still areas of difficult adjustment. Housing remains a problem, complicated by a general shortage in the face of population growth and shifts. Nor is the issue of segregation in education fully resolved. Nevertheless, the Supreme Court decision of 1954 has mapped the course of future development. In the District of Columbia and in Baltimore the change-over was prompt and smooth. In the border states of Delaware, Maryland, Missouri, Oklahoma, and West Virginia there has been substantial progress. Arkansas, Kentucky, and Tennessee have made encouraging steps in the direction of compliance; and only the eight states of the Deep South have actively resisted the trend. Even in those which have there is a growing awareness of the inevitability of the trend—"if not now, then in ten or fifteen years."

Few Americans today seriously believe segregation will remain a permanent part of American life. The pattern has been irretrievably destroyed. If Negroes may ride with whites in interstate trains and planes, it will be difficult to keep them apart on local transit lines; those who serve and live together in the armed forces will find it difficult to take up the ancient ways in civil life. Mississippi may continue to find a troglodyte to represent it in the Senate, but the species finds it ever more difficult to survive in the light. Even under the pressures of a presidential campaign in 1956 the white councils and similar organization were more moderate in tone than were their counterparts eight years earlier.

The forces of change have also eroded the lesser forms of segregation and discrimination based on differences of religion or national origin. Since the war such factors have, for all intents and purposes, been banned from political discussion. Every serious contender for public office hastens to make known his sentiments of tolerance and friendship toward all groups. True, the quota system to restrict immigration remains on the statute books. But the tone of controversy has dramatically altered; even such a hardened defender of the racist provisions as Congressman Walter must take his stand on the grounds that they are not racist and not discriminatory.

More important, whether with the aid of legislation or without, the practices of discrimination in employment, in education, and in social life have all but disappeared. Selection by quota in colleges, the Anglo-Saxon proviso in fraternity charters, the restricted resort or residential neighborhood, and gentlemen's agreements of various kinds have, with mounting frequency, been discarded as outmoded and anachronistic. American practice has come to accept the premise that all men are equal no matter what degrees of diversity divide them. In this sense it may no longer be appropriate at all to refer to "minorities."

It is immensely important to understand the nature of the changes that destroyed racism, the hate movements, and discrimination. The causes are complex—as complex as those which earlier brought the ugly manifestations of intolerance and hatred into our lives.

A variety of internal and external trends converged in the middle of the decade of the 1930's to produce a far-reaching revolution in the practice, the politics, and the theory of group life in America.

Most readily discernible was the example of Europe. Among all Americans there was unanimity in the shock at what transpired under the impact of fascism. Many early admirers of Mussolini were already disillusioned in 1933; Hitler completed the process even for those, in the United States, who should intellectually have been prepared for his doctrines and his actions. By the time war came in 1939, there could be no equivocation. This was a living image, the demonstration in actuality, of the goal toward which race theories led.

It was significant that Madison Grant's new book, published in 1933, evoked only ridicule and apathy, as if hundreds of thousands of readers had not seriously heeded his warnings little more than a decade before. It was no longer possible to read such writings innocently, to toy with the race theories as a kind of intellectual game. Nor could one now join a movement of ill-defined purposes merely for the sake of social cohesiveness; or, for that matter, choose among rival applicants for a job on the basis of vague, ill-defined preferences or dislikes. The results were all too obvious in Europe, and the connections increasingly plain. The example of the degradation of Germany, and the mounting revulsion in response to it, steadily turned Americans against the practices, the movements, and the ideas associated with fascism.

The shift was sustained by forces emanating from the

actual diversities in American life. The manifest differences
that actually divided the population gave the lie to every
effort to create or perpetuate a myth of American people-
hood in the sense of common descent. Even the efforts to
achieve some kind of unified direction among the scattered
fascist movements of the 1930's invariably proved abortive.
This was the fate of the plan in 1939 to unite the Knights
of the White Camelia with a variety of other organizations,
under the leadership of General George Van Horn Mose-
ley. No sooner were the various elements brought together
than they recognized they had nothing in common but their
hatreds; some of the anti-Semites were also anti-Catholic
and therefore incapable of collaborating with the followers
of Father Coughlin. German agents in the United States
who strove to effect a combination of forces could not comprehend this. They never grasped the fact that the genuine
plurality of American society prevented any exclusive movement from enlisting the support of more than a small
element of the total population.

A revived consciousness of the importance of the ideals
of equality and liberty also contributed to the change in
attitudes. Even during the decades of bitterest prejudice
the followers of the philosophers of pluralism, William
James and John Dewey, as well as a heartening number of
social workers and other citizens had resisted the dominant
trend toward racism. Such men drew support from a body
of ideas that went back to the eighteenth century and had
not altogether been submerged in 1900. Those ideas had
never been entirely without defenders. Even at the high
tide of racism, between 1890 and 1930, there had been
militant dissenters from the prevailing view who insisted
that the words of the Declaration of Independence had a
continuing and direct relevance to American life. Always
the "glittering generalities" of the Revolutionary period had
been remembered by some, and the respect due them remained an impediment in the way of those who wished to
deny the equality of man—not enough of an impediment
to prevent the development of racism, but enough to keep
alive a sense of discordance with tradition.

In the 1930's the reaction of the New Deal to the depression crisis strengthened the humanitarian ideals. Franklin Roosevelt and his most influential admirers were not, at the start, very greatly concerned with the problems of the minorities. Other issues seemed more important and the predominance of conservative Southerners in the leadership of the Democratic party made it wiser to evade such divisive issues. But, whether it willed it or not, the New Deal created an ideology; the President, no doubt, was vague in his intentions when he spoke of freedom and equality for the "forgotten man." But in doing so he aroused a general sense of obligation toward all forgotten men. Identifying the Jeffersonian elements in the American tradition with humanitarianism, the New Deal called attention to the values of equality of opportunity and increasingly focused attention upon the problems of the minorities.

As the decade advanced, the affiliation became closer. Huey Long and Father Coughlin broke with Roosevelt and that turned New Dealers against the type of movement the extremists represented. On the other hand, the administration had the support of an effective political alliance of minorities, and it gave an unprecedented number of high offices to the children and grandchildren of immigrants, to Catholics and Jews, aware of the problems of those groups.

There was a remarkable awakening of political consciousness among the minorities themselves in the 1930's. The trend began to take form after the shock of the prejudices displayed in the election of 1928. It gained strength as a new generation matured, less frightened than its predecessor and more insistent upon its rights. People who were electing aldermen and mayors and congressmen were ever less likely to accept the role of second-class citizens.

The minorities were prepared to act because the free institutions of the United States had afforded them the opportunity to organize a coherent group life of their own. By 1928 the churches, the benevolent and fraternal societies, and associations for self-defense constituted a force to be reckoned with. Furthermore, it had become clear to all these groups that they could secure their own rights best by fighting for the common rights of all. The consciousness that Jews, Catholics, and Negroes have an identical stake in freedom because they were once together the objects of prejudice has a continuing importance in the adjustments of the present and the future. It explains, for example, why Mobile, Alabama, has fewer problems of desegregation than Montgomery, in the same state.

The minorities were able to take organized action because American institutions left substantial areas of social life free from interference by the state. In those areas voluntary association was traditional, accepted and recognized by constitutional guarantees. Many societies cut across group lines and created fields of common action. It is notable, for example, that the veterans' organizations, however shortsighted they may have been in other respects, did not in the United States, as their counterparts did in Europe, lend themselves to the plots of the hate movements. Even in the 1920's the community funds, the Red Cross, and other voluntary agencies were learning the value of cooperative effort.

The freedoms that limited the government's capacity to control the individual exercised a decisive restraint upon the Klan and its successors. None of these groups could take effective political action, for they were incapable of formulating specific programs and could only indulge in demagogic generalities because the secured rights of the individual narrowly circumscribed what the government could do. Occasional laws which went beyond these limits, as in the efforts to proscribe parochial schools, were struck down by the courts. Significantly the greatest obstacle to further progress today is the persistence of informal practices which are contrary to the spirit of American democracy. The Senate seniority system and misrepresentative districting in the state legislatures are notable examples.

The wider context of American society has, however, been favorable. General prosperity since the Second World War and the disappearance of unemployment have eased the immediate strains of competition for places far more than under the comparable conditions of the 1920's. The economic well-being of the last decade has been accompanied by a general relaxation of tensions which may have enormous consequences for the future. The emphasis upon personal adjustment and security and the development of a wide range of permissive habits have restored a measure of stability to family life. Reflections of that stability appear in the rapidly rising birth rate, in the development of suburban life, and in the general diffusion of middle-class tastes and values through the whole society. The yearning for respectability and order may entail other losses, but it has given millions of Americans a sense of purpose and goal that leaves them less subject to the old fears and hatreds which earlier made strangers of their neighbors.

Finally, there has been a radical change in science and in the popular view of science. The most direct result was a greater understanding in the 1930's and 1940's of prejudice and of the means of its abatement. Programs for easing intergroup hostility and for intercultural education were practical manifestations of important changes in genetics, in psychology, in anthropology, in sociology, and in the historical interpretation of the American past. In the face of those changes it might well have been asked, "What happened to race?"

Americans still open the morning newspaper to encounter the troubling problems of prejudice. An outbreak of violence in Cicero, Hawaii's difficulty in attaining statehood, or a lost election in North Carolina reveals what a way yet remains to be traveled before the heritage of old hatreds disappears.

But the backward look is encouraging. In the past twenty years our society has experienced a veritable revolution, scarcely noticed by those who participated in it. The experience of Europe, the actual diversity of our people, and the strength of our free institutions provided the instruments for destroying the inequalities of practice and theory that made minorities of some of us.

CHAPTER VIII

What Happened to Race?

SCIENCE, which created race as an intellectual concept, also helped destroy it. For it is the strength of science to contain within itself the means of its own redemption. The dedication to truth which animates the scholar's inquiry, again and again, brings him back to a reinvestigation of the evidence. Respect for the evidence raises in each man's mind questions as to the interpretations he builds upon it. The process of re-examination acquired more importance than ever before as scientists became aware of the degree to which their own preconceptions influenced their conclusions.

The result was a complete revision of the basic ideas upon which the old notion of race rested. The scholarship of the past thirty years has touched at many points upon the matters dealt with in the Dillingham and the Laughlin reports. It has coped far more adequately with the patterns of prejudice and the problems of race, with the course of immigration through American history, with the nature of the economic and social adjustments of migrants, and with the extent to which intelligence, education, crime, insanity, and other social disorders vary among the diverse groups of the American population. Large areas, of course, still remain open for investigation, and at some places the evidence is inconclusive. But enough data is available to permit a fresh evaluation of the fundamental conceptions to which the Dillingham Commission gave expression forty-five years ago. Such a revaluation will show the distance science has traveled since.

1. GENETICS AND THE NATURE OF RACE

Intensive research into the problems of heredity has led to a much clearer understanding of how physical traits are transmitted across the generations. In so doing the theories both of Darwin and Galton have been abandoned. The new point of departure has been the observations of an Austrian abbot who patiently tended the rows of peas in his garden. Johann Mendel, called Gregor when he became an Augustinian monk, published his conclusions in 1866; but the decades that followed were not congenial to his views, which lay disregarded for more than thirty years. Then in 1900 their relevance became compellingly clear to a number of scholars, and modern genetics is the result.

Such physical traits as the color of the eyes or hair and the pigmentation of the skin do pass through the genes from parents to children. The carriers have been identified and described. We know now that a group of individuals with common characteristics will procreate offspring with the same characteristics. Mankind is composed of a variety of populations which differ among themselves in the frequency of many genes. These Mendelian populations will reproduce themselves across time.

But these Mendelian populations differ in two critical respects from what earlier geneticists called races. They are not identical with the national, linguistic, religious, economic, or other cultural groupings into which mankind is also divided. These overlap and cut across each other's boundaries. "People with blue eyes, or with round or with oblong heads, or with heads shaped like some prehistoric skull, or fat people or people convicted for crime, or sufferers from cancer or other diseases do not form Mendelian populations." The attempt to conflate the various categories can only yield meaningless confusion.

Furthermore, the Mendelian population is not fixed, but undergoes evolutionary changes. It may split into several distinct populations, or several quite separate ones may fuse into one. A variety of social and cultural factors may break down or create gene pools. Therefore the existence of such a grouping at a given point in time is not in itself evidence of the common descent of its members any more than it establishes the presumption that their descendants will still be part of the same population. This is certainly a far cry from the conception of race as a fixed category, united by common descent and social as well as physical characteristics.

"Race" as a term is still useful, if properly defined. A helpful statement prepared for UNESCO by a group of distinguished biologists, psychologists, and social scientists in 1950 outlines the points upon which there was a general consensus of opinion. Its central conclusions may be stated as follows:

Mankind is essentially one, descended from the same common stock. The species is divided into a number of populations, or races, which differ from each other in the frequency of one or more genes which determine the hereditary concentration of physical traits. Those traits are not fixed, but may appear, fluctuate, and disappear in the course of time. It is presently possible to distinguish three such races—the Mongoloid, the Negroid, and the Caucasoid —but no subgroups within them can be meaningfully described in physical terms. National, religious, geographic, linguistic, and cultural groups do not coincide with race, and the cultural and social traits of such groups have no genetic connection with racial traits. There is no evidence of any inborn differences of temperament, personality, character, or intelligence among races.

Therefore it follows that the only meaningful basis upon which one can compare social and cultural traits is in terms of the ethnic group, which preserves its continuity to the extent that its culture passes from generation to generation through a common social environment. The inheritance of an ethnic group consists not of its biological characteristics, but of its culture.

Modern anthropology has therefore devoted more attention than was usual in earlier years to the study of cultural rather than physical differences, both in preliterate and in our own societies. These differences are viewed as the product of habits, attitudes, beliefs, and institutions developed in the course of adjustments to their environment, broadly construed, by individuals and cultural groups. Differences of this sort may persist over very long periods of time, but they are not determined by the physical traits of the men marked off by them.

Since race in the old sense is no longer an important consideration, it will be enlightening to consider the effects of persisting cultural differences upon our society, primarily in terms of the place within it of the numerous ethnic groups of which it is formed. It may be, in time, that the Negroes will still constitute a distinct group, but one marked off by its own heritage rather than by the prejudice attached to its color. Regarding the problem from that perspective, we have learned much in recent years about the effect on the nation of the heterogeneity and plurality of its population.

2. MIGRATION AND THE ETHNIC GROUPS IN AMERICAN LIFE

Diverse ethnic groups played a particularly important role in American history. In the United States the government always left large areas of social action free for the activities of voluntary organizations. Without any compulsion toward uniformity individuals associated with one another in religious, social, philanthropic, cultural, and economic organizations, through which they preserved the distinctive differences that separated them from other Americans. These differences originated in a number of factors. Religion, for instance, was the basis of identification among such groups as the Mormons or Quakers or Jews. Color set the Negroes and Japanese apart. Most important, immigration, which brought to the United States men of diverse cultural antecedents, left them in groups based upon their common heritages, interests, and ideas.

Immigration therefore always played a central role in the formation of American culture. From the very first settlement it helped shape the distinctive institutions of the nation. The effects of immigration, as those are now understood, may therefore offer a clue to the continuing role of the ethnic group in the United States.

The most important contributions to the understanding of this process in recent years have emphasized its continuity. Exceptional men have often enriched our culture— the East Anglican Puritans, the forty-eighters, or the refugee scientists of the 1930's. But the mass of people who arrived in the seventeenth century were not substantially different from those who came in the eighteenth or in the nineteenth or in the twentieth. Although each of the ethnic groups which reached the New World had its distinctive cultural and social life, and although they were at different stages of development at the point of departure, the process that brought them all was the same. Their social origins and their motives were always very much alike.

It is therefore no longer possible to speak of meaningful distinctions between settlers and immigrants or between old and new immigrants. Englishmen, Germans, Italians, and Poles spoke different languages, had different habits, and were accustomed to different forms of behavior. But the kinds of Englishmen who came to the United States in the seventeenth and eighteenth centuries were very much the same as the kinds of Irish, Germans, and Scandinavians who came in the middle of the nineteenth, and these in turn were very much like the Italians, Jews, and Poles who came later.

Very largely all these immigrants were people displaced by economic changes in the structure of modern agriculture and industry. With the growth of population and with the mechanization of industry and agriculture large numbers of artisans found their handicrafts useless and even larger numbers of peasants found no place for themselves on the land. These were the people to whom opportunity beckoned in the New World. The generating economic changes began in England and spread to the east; that accounts for the difference in the era at which various peoples began to migrate. But the process was one and continuous.

In discussing adjustment to life in the United States it is therefore necessary to take account of both similarities and differences among the groups involved. To some extent the qualities of the cultural heritage influenced the course of that adjustment. But more important was the nature of the opportunities open to the immigrant and the length of time afforded him for adjustment. In no case does the line between old and new seem significant.

3. THE ECONOMIC ADJUSTMENT

Properly or not, discussion of the problems of immigration has often focused on the nature of the effects on the economy. The Immigration Commission devoted the bulk of its labors to this subject, and for some Americans this has been the decisive aspect of the question. Scholarly studies have thrown considerable light on the effects of immigration on depressions, on wages, on occupational stratification and mobility, and on economic innovations.

a. *Immigration and depressions.* It was once feared that immigration, which added new hands to the labor supply, contributed to the severity of depressions. The evidence of the depression that followed the panic of 1929 points in the other direction. In the early 1930's the volume of unemployment remained high and the depression intense despite the complete curtailment of immigration. These phenomena depended upon the more general fluctuations of the business cycle rather than upon a single factor, immigration.

Furthermore, studies of the period of free migration down to 1924 have indicated the likelihood that immigration may actually have eased the effects of depression. The volume of immigration seemed to rise sharply during periods of prosperity and to sink rapidly in periods of depression. Such shifts lent fluidity to the labor supply, enabling it to expand when more hands were needed and to contract when they were not.

b. *Immigration and wages.* In the years of argument over restriction some Americans feared that immigration would tend to drive wages downward. There were some grounds for that uneasiness. As a theoretical proposition it seemed

convincing that the effect of adding to the supply of labor
was to drive down its cost. Furthermore, through much of
the period of free immigration the average *real* wages of
labor, particularly of unskilled labor, fell or were stationary.

Examined more closely, however, the relationship of immigration to labor assumes another appearance. A simple
comparison of the conditions of labor in 1900 with those in
1850 has little value for this purpose. To deal with the
over-all average for labor, including all unskilled labor, is
not very informative as to the effects of immigration on
the pre-existing labor force, because the immigrants themselves come to constitute a large part of the sample. Only
by eliminating from the account the unskilled labor of the
immigrants can one assess the effects of the arrival upon
the natives. Such a reckoning reveals that the fate of skilled
native workers improved steadily in the period of immigration. Furthermore, the coming of the immigrants, by
broadening the range of opportunities at the top of the
occupational ladder, actually lifted the earlier labor force
to higher job levels and thus increased their income. As
long as the whole economy was expansive, therefore, immigration probably raised rather than lowered the wage
level of existing laborers.

In the more recent past, with wages largely set by collec-
tive bargaining, the decisive element in the determination
of wage rates has been the state of labor organization in
any given industry. When the opportunity has been afforded them, immigrants have shown their readiness to join
unions in defense of their interests as workers. Given the
continued capacity of the economy to expand in the future,
a moderate amount of immigration seems no threat either
to wage rates or to the unions.

c. *Immigration and occupational stratification.* Although
economic opportunities in American society were open to
all, some groups were more likely than others to take
advantage of them. The determining factors were complex, with some, although not all of them, related to
immigration.

Most immigrants entered the American economy at the

lowest levels, primarily as unskilled laborers. This was the logical outcome of the situation of peasants arriving in an industrial society without capital. The lack of skill and the initial role as laborers were characteristic of the old immigrants as of the new, of the Irish and Germans as of the Italians and Poles, although the proportions differed somewhat. There were occasional exceptions, of course, as among the British immigrants of the last quarter of the nineteenth century and among the Jews a little later.

It seems clear that the occupational level of all such groups rose with the passage of time, although no general study has as yet examined with sufficient care the means through which that rise occurred or the factors which affected its rate. The groups varied considerably in their experiences, and those variations no doubt reflected differences in cultural background as well as in the availability of opportunities and the length of settlement.

That the factor last named was often crucial was shown by the findings in a survey of Newburyport, Massachusetts. Using indexes of their own contriving, the authors of that study traced the occupational status of eight ethnic groups over nine decades, from 1850 to 1933. They discovered that almost all groups raised their status in time, that relative position tended to vary with duration of settlement, and that some new immigrants (Armenians and Jews, for example) did better than the old Irish. Scattered data on home ownership and savings accounts in general supported the same conclusions.

d. *Innovations and immigration.* Finally, the possibility must not be overlooked that among any group of immigrants or their children there may be an occasional individual who by his gifts as an outsider becomes one of the long list of innovators, inventors, or entrepreneurs who have helped to stimulate American industry in the past. No test will reveal which particular group will in the future bring along a Michael Pupin, a Conrad Huber, an Ottmar Mergenthaler, or a Giuseppe Bellanca. But a society will make best use of such talented individuals if it offers them the opportunity to rise to the status at which they can use their ability, whatever their origin.

To sum up, the adverse effects of immigration seem to have been slight, the gains for Americans and newcomers considerable. All the groups which have hitherto immigrated have had some economic difficulties in the sense that they have had to begin with the poorest jobs, but all have shown the capacity to thrive from the opportunities of American life.

4. INTELLIGENCE AND ADJUSTMENT

Among the indexes that have conventionally been used to judge the capacity of various ethnic groups for Americanization were their intelligence and education. These were long the ostensible justifications for the literacy test since, it was argued, only the fittest groups ought to be permitted to assume the responsibilities of American citizenship.

The difficulty was to find a reliable basis for comparing the intelligence of diverse groups. The Army intelligence tests of 1917 and 1918 were inconclusive since they did not eliminate from the results the effect of differences of environment. All that could reliably be deduced from these tests was that duration of residence was a significant factor. Beyond that there was no sound basis for establishing valid differences in intelligence among various ethnic groups.

There is a good deal of evidence of difference in educational attainment. Local data indicates that some groups are more proficient in their schooling and advance to higher grades than others. Ethnic values and background may be conditioning factors here. On the other hand, there is also evidence that the social environment is critical. Negro children who migrate from the South to the North thus show a marked rise in intelligence quotient. Furthermore, a general study of American education has shown that the most significant variable in the ability of children to profit from their schooling is the character of the social environment and the class from which they come. In all this material there is little to suggest that any group is innately incapable of being Americanized by reason of deficiencies in its intelligence.

5. CRIMINALITY AND ADJUSTMENT

Very similar conclusions emerge from the studies of criminality in the past twenty-five years. As to total inclination to crime the (Wickersham) National Commission on Law Observance and Enforcement found that the foreign-born committed fewer crimes than the native-born in proportion to their respective numbers in the total population. This result is plausible enough, although there must always be a good deal of difficulty in compensating for differences due to the social distribution of the groups concerned.

The commission also felt that among the foreign-born there seemed to be variations, from group to group, in the proneness to commit certain types of crimes. But its evidence, it feared, was not adequate to sustain any firm generalization.

A more recent study tended to confirm the predilection of various ethnic groups to certain types of crimes. Professor E. A. Hooton (*Crime and the Man* [Cambridge, 1939]) found that crime was not due to influences generated by race or ethnic affiliations. But given a criminal individual, the type of crime committed was likely to be determined by the character of the group from which he sprang. Certainly this factor is, in general, minor in comparison with the other social, psychological, and biological elements affecting the rate of criminality in the United States.

Juvenile delinquency now also seems less a concomitant of immigration or ethnic affiliation than formerly. Intensive investigations have not found conclusive evidence that the children of immigrants are more likely to be delinquent than the children of natives; and given equality of social environment, there is even an indication they may be less so.

Furthermore, there is now a sound basis for believing that the cultural conflict deriving from ethnic affiliations is of only slight importance in determining the incidence of juvenile delinquency, and that the more critical factors spring from the social and family environment and from the personality of the individual child.

The total trend of these investigations has been to minimize the possible influence upon criminality of immigration or of ethnic background. Certainly they supply no grounds for the fear that the new immigrants were likely to be more dangerous than the old, or the Negroes more prone to lawbreaking than the whites.

6. ALCOHOLISM AND ADJUSTMENT

Statistical measurement of the incidence of alcoholism offered the same difficulties as that of other disorders. The data was at best partial and had to be adjusted against deviations with care. Thus figures for arrests for drunkenness were not very useful since these varied enormously from place to place and were likely to affect almost exclusively the lowest social groups.

A somewhat more reliable index, though hardly a thoroughly dependable one, was the rate of commitment for alcoholic psychoses in state institutions. This offered the advantage of a relatively constant criterion and one that could be fairly well standardized. A study of New York State institutions in the 1930's used this index with good results (Benjamin Malzberg, *Social and Biological Aspects of Mental Disease* [Utica, 1940], 163 ff.). That study found that the foreign-born had a rate of 7.4 per 100,000 population while the native rate was only 3.2. But standardized to remove the influence of different age distributions, the disparity disappeared almost entirely, with the foreign and native rates nearly equal.

The distribution by specific nativity groups was striking for it showed marked variations as significant as the equality of the over-all foreign with the native rate. The maximum was for the Irish with 30.5, followed by the Scandinavians with 7.9, the English with 4.8, the Italians, 4.3, and the Germans, 3.8. Whether these differences reflected some sort of ethnic predilection or whether they reflected differences in the social environment would be difficult to judge in the absence of any convincing theory as to the causes of alcoholism. Perhaps the most that could be said is that the immigrants as a whole did not add to the burden of the problem, although specific groups among them may have. But those groups could by no means be correlated with the old and new immigrations.

7. INSANITY

On the basis of summary rates of commitment or of first admissions it was sometimes maintained that insanity was more frequent among the foreign-born than among the native-born. A careful study has shown, however, "that such comparisons are spurious, in that they fail to account for the effects of age and other disturbing conditions." The foreign-born are older than the natives and "consequently tend to have higher rates of first admissions." Furthermore, the foreign-born are more concentrated in cities, from which the rates of commitment are higher. "When age and the urban-rural ratio are both held constant," there is practically no significant difference between the foreign- and the native-born.

Dr. Malzberg's study found instead a correlation between the incidence of insanity and "general economic conditions." To the extent that that conclusion was valid, immigration has had no perceptible effect upon the general rate of insanity.

The problem was more complicated, however. For, as in the case of alcoholism, there has been a marked disparity in the incidence of the disease among various nativity groups, with the Irish far in the lead. Furthermore, if the various types of psychoses were differentiated, it appeared that the Scandinavians were ahead in admissions for general paresis, while the Germans were in the lead in admissions for dementia praecox.

A study of draft-board rejections for mental disorders confirmed these findings (Robert W. Hyde and Roderick M. Chisholm, "The Relation of Mental Disorders to Race and Nationality," *New England Journal of Medicine*, CCXXXI [1944], 612 ff.). This study had the advantage of dealing with ethnic (second generation as well as foreign-born) rather than simply with nativity groups. It showed convincingly a difference in the susceptibility of various groups to different types of mental disorder. In view of the fact that the total foreign-born rate was not larger than the total native-born, immigration seemed to offer no threat of increased incidence of insanity in the whole population. And in view of the difficulty of establishing a ranking of the various groups that would be valid for all types of insanity, it was futile to attempt to use this as one of the elements of selection of immigrants.

From what has been said above, there seems to be the following general pattern to what we know about the problems of insanity, alcoholism, crime, and intelligence:

There is no evidence that the immigrants have been inferior to the natives, no evidence that the new immigrants have been inferior to the old, and no evidence that immigration has produced any social deterioration in the United States.

None of these relationships is based on race. All may be radically altered under the impact of the changing environment of life in the United States, and all vary to some extent with the duration of residence.

For each of the disorders mentioned there was some evidence of variation among different groups of immigrants; but no immigrant group, old or new, ranked consistently high or consistently low in all the categories. These variations, therefore, were not such as to make it possible to rank the groups in order of desirability. Significantly there was also no evidence that relative distance from American culture was a factor of any importance in determining ultimate adjustment. That is, people like the Syrians, Armenians, and Turks, relatively more alien to native American habits and ways of life, were not significantly retarded in adjustment, given the time and opportunity. The evidence suggests rather that, like the native population, each immigrant group had its own points of strength and weakness at which it yielded to, or resisted, disorganizing pressures that originated in the environment or in personal disturbances. No group was thereby prevented from playing a constructive part in American life.

8. CITIZENSHIP

There was some disposition early in the century to criticize the new immigrants for the failure to be naturalized; the Immigration Commission, for one, lent its support to such criticism. These attacks uniformly failed to consider the factor of length of residence in the United States. When account was taken of that factor, the old immigration made no better showing than the new. A study of the percentage of foreign-born naturalized as of 1940 revealed that the various nativity groups could be ranked in an order which corresponded almost exactly with the average length of residence in the United States (F. J. Brown and J. S. Roucek, *One America* [New York, 1945], 657). The only exceptions were the natives of England and British Canada, who showed unusual reluctance to become American citizens. These findings were indirectly supported by an earlier study of New Haven, which showed a correlation of naturalization with education, occupational status, and income—concomitants generally of length of residence.

Nor has there been evidence that the immigrants, or any group of them, have shirked the important duties of citizenship. The two world wars in which the United States engaged in the last forty years found these men ready to serve; their part in the armed services has been fully documented and often recognized.

9. CULTURAL CONTRIBUTIONS

An evaluation of the social experience of the immigrants to the United States must also take some account of their positive contributions to American culture. It would be pointless, however, to attempt to assess the relative merits of one group as against another. The more significant conclusion that emerges from the survey of American art, music, literature, science, theater, and sports is that every group has shown the capacity to produce individuals able to play a useful role in such endeavors. The distinctions between old and new immigrants, in retrospect, seem quite pointless. There was no basis for predicting which among the millions of men and women who landed on our shores would themselves or through their children bring the gifts that contributed to American culture. It seems certain only that without these contributions life in the United States in the past would have been far poorer than it was. In a more subtle sense the most valuable contribution of the immigrants, old and new, was always to remind Americans of the motto on the great seal, *E Pluribus Unum*, from many one. Their adjustment involved the achievement of unity—and yet the preservation of diversities—in American society.

What has been true of the ethnic groups set off by immigration is also true of those distinguishable by their color. A point-by-point examination of the social and cultural characteristics of the American Negroes leads to the identical conclusion as with regard to the immigrants. The black man's traits are not identical with those of the whites, just as various white groups are not identical with each other. But all those differences are primarily the products of influences emanating from the social and cultural milieu. They are not related to the physical nature of the Negro and they constitute no barrier in the way of his occupying a fully equal place in American life.

The whole scientific basis for the race fears and hatred of the past has thus disappeared. That does not mean, of course, that all the fears and hatreds themselves have vanished any more than the terror of the nightmare with the waking. But the light does bring reassurance, and there is room for hope that a deeper understanding of prejudice and of its psychological, social, and historical sources will help to dissipate its effects.

That would leave America free to confront the challenges of its diverse society. For the groupings within it which have so often presented problems in the past may as often create opportunities for the future. There are encouraging indications in our own experience of the means by which those opportunities may be exploited.

Potentialities

CHAPTER IX

The Larger Significance

THE CENTRAL problem of the free society is the orderly conduct of its communal institutions on some basis other than an authoritarian one. The modern state has at hand the massive instruments of compulsion created by high technology and speedy communications. In the absence of alternatives needy or desperate or grasping men will be tempted to summon the power of government to serve their own ends. The habit of reliance upon force, unchecked, has enlisted the unaware in the totalitarian causes of our times; and the weakness of autonomous voluntary institutions in many parts of the world has permitted monolithic regimes to dominate all human life and, in so doing, to stifle the liberties of the people.

The free societies which have been spared or have emerged from the trial of authoritarianism therefore face the constant obligation of understanding the institutions through which they function. It is not enough to proclaim that that government is best which governs least. The necessities of an era in which the mass is determining will not permit state power to lie idle where want and inequity are widespread. A proclamation more appropriate to the present would be that that government is best which has the least occasion to govern by virtue of the fact that other agencies serve the demands of the people for justice and the public welfare.

With regard to those demands the contemporary crisis is the product of long-term changes which prevent the family from performing functions for which it traditionally took the responsibility. Through the whole history of Western society the family was the focal point of social organization. Although the institution itself passed through a variety of forms in the centuries of its development, it long supplied the masses of men with security available nowhere else. The emotional satisfactions, the sensations of personal stability, and the consciousness of continuity through the generations attached to it a complex of loyalties and devotions.

Through most of its history the family existed in a relatively fixed and stable social setting. Often it was associated with political force; under feudalism and, indeed, down to our own era it was a determining element in the disposition of the power to govern. Again it was intimately connected with the religious rite; it was the instrumentality through which the oncoming generations were initiated into the communion, were brought to an acquaintance with the right, were married and in turn created their own families and ultimately found their death and passed away. Finally, the family was the key element in the tenure of property and in its transmission from generation to generation. In these multiple relationships the family was a source of stability and of continuing order. At the same time external relationships fortified and vitalized the ties among its membership. Kinship involved not merely consanguinity, but also the complex of religious, economic, and political associations.

In the early history of modern Europe, thus, the family was the essential channel of social order. Status was acquired, held, and passed on through it. Among the feudal nobility and their descendants property, rank, and power passed in accord with its tables of descent. Among the peasantry it was also the unit of agricultural production. And even in the cities the guilds and, down to very recent times, the conduct of extensive business operations depended on the same range of connections.

The critical role of these relationships was characteristic also of occasional groups considered outsiders in the dominant society. Among the Jews, for example, genealogy often carried weighty influence, and that was likewise the case among the Huguenot émigrés from France, among the dissenters of England, and among the German settlers in Russia. Such groups adapted the family patterns of the majority to their own situation.

In the lives of all these people the unsettlement of traditional family relationships evoked a long and difficult process of readjustment. That unsettlement began slowly in the sixteenth and seventeenth centuries with the crumbling away of the external institutions with which the family had been intertwined. The old feudal order disintegrated, the unity of the church disappeared, the forms of agricultural production changed, and commercial and business habits took on a new aspect. The pace varied from place to place and from time to time, but the transformation has not yet come to a halt.

Often, particularly among the prosperous classes capable of preserving the old values and with the means of protecting their resources, the family retained vestiges of its former importance. But sooner or later it proved incapable of resisting the pressures of an environment increasingly hostile to it. Democracy, the diffuse society of the metropolis, and the impersonal qualities of factory industry tended to treat the individual isolated from any other attachment. What remained were the personalities of husbands and wives, of parents and children. The continuing strains these circumstances created called for great personal and emotional sacrifices. The result was a prolonged period of tension, the end of which is not yet in sight.

The crisis was extreme in those areas and under such conditions as compelled the family to adjust at once to a completely new round of economic and social behavior. The pressure of industrialization was often totally disruptive to all existing patterns of life. As the cities of Europe and America grew in the nineteenth century, they pulled into their orbits millions of displaced and totally unprepared peasants. The host of proletarians who gathered around the new factories lacked the material or spiritual or emotional resources to deal with their new situation. It was more extreme still when the transition from rural to urban existence involved at the same time migration to a totally strange culture. There the adjustment was most difficult.

Men could not live in disorder. They struggled for reconstruction, hoping to regain the values lost in the disintegration of family life. Or, if the old ways could not be restored, they longed to create new kinds of groupings that might compensate for their loss by supplying a new kind of solidarity. In the United States the effort proceeded under conditions created by the contact of a diverse population and by the relative freedom and equality of the social order. In Australia the adjustment was dominated by the fact that the great mass of immigrants were drawn from a single source, the British Isles. In Brazil a more stable society dealt with the process in another way. And, more recently, in Israel the desire to find new attachments for the values left unstable by changes in the family was influenced by the common religion of the immigrants and by an ancient Messianic dream. Each of these societies attempted to mold into new forms the impulses that could no longer be contained in the old. Therein the immigrant lands were not different in kind, but in degree, from those long settled.

Three alternatives unfolded before those who sought compensation for their unsatisfied needs. One way led toward racism; belief in a common biological descent from which others were excluded offered men a reflection of the unity they now missed in the family. That belief had tragic consequences and, in any case, has proved delusive.

Another alternative was to consider the state a comprehensive community capable of attaching to itself the loyalties and emotions of its citizens. The involvement of the masses of men in government incapacitated the dynastic rulers of the past. Their successors, whether in a democracy or dictatorship, used power in the name of the people, and the people's response was nationalism.

This was a sentiment particularly attractive to intellectuals, detached men, who found it a means of establishing a rapport they otherwise lacked with a community that gave their own lives broader meaning and purpose. It took longer and was more difficult to establish the attraction of the state for people who still thought back to the family and the village as the communal units. The process often involved the creation of new national entities and the elaboration of myths that established their roots in the past.

There were times when nationalism had an ennobling quality. For Mazzini and the European liberals of the mid-nineteenth century it was an instrument for the diffusion of freedom and the destruction of tyranny. For the generation of the American Revolution it was the means by which the New World was to redress the balances of the Old; their mission was to develop the forms of democracy that would enlighten and redeem all mankind. In such contexts its visions were broad and cosmopolitan.

From the latter part of the nineteenth century onward, however, nationalism was also susceptible to distortion by racist assumptions. Race supplied those who sought it with the myth of common identity and unity, and the belief in blood ties was equally attractive to intellectuals and to the masses for its scientific and emotional satisfactions. But the price was cruel: nationalism then had to exclude the stranger and it demanded total conformity within the community. It thus could be aggressive in the face of the outside world and destructive of the liberties of its own kind.

The third alternative for those who sought a sense of belonging could also be linked with nationalism, but in another way. The modern state, short of totalitarianism, did not pre-empt all the fields of social action. A variety of concerns differing from place to place remained in the hands of voluntary associations. Among these concerns might be religion, education, philanthropy, and recreation —all matters with which the family had once been preoccupied, and in which it was still involved.

In a free society such as the United States the groups which devoted themselves to such nongovernmental functions tended to follow an ethnic pattern. Men with common antecedents and ideas were usually disposed to join together to further their religious, charitable, and social interests through churches and a multitude of other organizations; and through such activities many individuals became conscious of the fact that, while they were all

Americans, some were also Swedes or Jews or Dutch or Quakers.

The strength of the ethnic group lay in its freedom and its fluidity. Its members identified themselves with it not through external compulsion, but rather because it served their needs. If it did not, they were able to withdraw and sometimes even to establish new identifications. Furthermore, the ethnic group made no exclusive demands upon the loyalty of the individuals who composed it. The man who acted as an Italian when he met with the Sons of Italy was not thereby deprived of the capacity for being a good Catholic or Episcopalian when he went to church, or a good union member when he met with his local, or a good American in the polling booth.

Finally, the ethnic group provided a context within which family ties acquired a renewed function. The group itself existed through the willingness of children to recognize and be identified with their parents. Yet by ordering some important aspects of the family's life it tended to hold together those who might otherwise be cast adrift without direction. So long as it was not restrictive, authoritarian, and exclusive, it provided the means for satisfying significant personal and emotional needs without arbitrary restraints or external compulsion.

Throughout the world these alternatives still confront millions of men the disruption of whose family life leads them to seek other forms of order.

The tragic consequences of racism are clear enough to most Europeans and Americans who were once deluded by it. Those results would be more tragic still were they to evoke a reciprocal racism among the colored people who were formerly its most abject victims.

We have seen something also, in recent decades, of the perils of unrestrained nationalism made the vehicle of totalitarian dictatorship. Our own history and the history of European liberalism, however, remind us that the loyalties and emotional responses called for by the state need not necessarily lend themselves to exploitation in this fashion. Rather, they can be the basis of a humanitarian international order within which different countries co-operate with and understand, but do not oppress, one another. The development of such an order may be far away, but nationalism as such does not stand in its way.

There remains the problem, however, of supplying the emotional and personal needs of the individual in such a manner that he will not be tempted to lose himself in blind identification with a total state or mythical race. To this problem the experience of American ethnic groups is germane.

The United States, by the uniqueness of its diverse society, once seemed an experiment of universal significance. The New World enjoyed, after all, the opportunity to avoid the errors of the Old. There was much in that experiment of which to be proud. There were some features of it in which no pride could be taken. It is never too soon to recall the former, and never too late to eliminate the latter. No task is more imperative than to remove from our lives segregation and the national-origins quota, two tenacious relics of racism which deny our own national ideals.

Segregation is the pattern of legal and social restraints that prevents Negroes from taking a place as one among many ethnic groups. Segregation, which is, at root, a form of compulsion, destroys the voluntary quality of identification and imposes on these people the odium of inferiority. In its absence the Negroes, equal in rights, might achieve an adjustment that would permit them to co-operate creatively with the other ethnic groups of which America is composed. Only fears inherited from a generation which wished, through race, to preserve the heritage of slavery stand in the way.

It is the same with the quota system. In the past the image of America had also a meaning for the common people of the whole world. It was not only that the United States was the land of liberty, in its form of government and free society a model for all other peoples. In our willingness to accept the persecuted and oppressed we also gave concrete evidence of our faith in the ability of all men to raise themselves to the same levels of freedom, as well as evidence of confidence in our own institutions.

The men who enacted the quota system lost that confidence. The same legislators also rejected the League of Nations, and they had the support of the public opinion that, through the 1920's, also favored American withdrawal from world politics. All these measures were aspects of a common urge, understandable in the light of the disappointments of the war and the peace, but unrealistic in terms of the future. That urge was to withdraw from all contacts with the evil world beyond the borders. The immigrants who carried that foreign world to these shores, from this viewpoint, threatened American isolation. The feat of dividing the immigrants into old and new was a device, presumably justified by science, in distinguishing the good from the bad. And the system of national-origins quotas, based upon that division, was the means of attaining a kind of security in isolation.

Certainly it would be foolhardy to take those old dead racist dreams as our vision of the future. We are totally and inextricably involved with the politics of the whole world; and the welfare and opinions of many strange peoples, from Korea in the west to Turkey in the east, are our immediate direct concern. We need only look at our foreign-aid budget to know how important to us is the prosperity of Greece and Italy. If our immigration policy can, in the least measure, assist those countries in dealing with the problems of displacement and recovery, we would be shortsighted in the extreme to allow ancient prejudices to stand in our way.

By the same token we shall be frustrating ourselves if we permit segregation to sap our own strength any longer than necessary. By such arbitrary divisions we prevent ourselves from applying our resources to best effect, from using talents where they can best serve, and from achieving the unity of spirit that comes from the knowledge that our practice is in accord with our principles.

More important, we are engaged throughout the world in a struggle for allies against a shrewd and ruthless enemy who does not hesitate to make millennial promises. In this contest for the control of opinions we enjoy an initial advantage derived from the reputation we earned as the mother of republics, the light of liberty, and the refuge of the oppressed throughout the world. We must not waste that advantage.

Segregation and the quota system threaten to do so. By ranking the people of the earth in an order of national origins our immigration law informs them that some are more fit to become Americans than others. Our treatment of the Negro too often confirms that. And that raises an uneasy question in their minds: Is our belief in democracy coupled with the reservation that it is workable only in favored climes and in the hands of favored men, or is this a way of life open to all?

The national-origins quota system and segregation rest on totally false assumptions. They are the products of men who lost confidence. With their uneasy fears they sought refuge in a kind of withdrawal from the world about them, hoping for security in the purity of their own race. Out of the biased science of the early part of this century they drew the distorted notion of a fundamental difference between black and white, between old and new immigrants. From that notion there followed the idea that different groups of men enjoyed different capacities for becoming American citizens.

Our own experience and everything we have learned since the 1930's refute that idea. We no longer believe race purity a safe refuge; we know it to be a trap dividing people arbitrarily and distracting them from solution of their true problems. Our economy and our society have continued to grow, and show even now the vigor to profit from the equality of all our citizens, and even from the addition of worthy new ones.

We also see more clearly what the role of free ethnic groups has been in our lives. Although these have differed among themselves, all have displayed from the very beginning of our history the ability to play a creative, constructive role in American society. They can continue to do so in the future. Given the opportunity, they may still contribute to the value, for all men, of the American experiment.

CHAPTER X

The Newest Immigrants

THE HISTORY of immigration in the recent experience of the United States offers a series of striking paradoxes. On the one hand, official policy, as expressed in legislation, has given only grudging tolerance to the newcomers. On the other, the reception accorded the new arrivals has been extremely favorable, and the actual process of settlement has been free of the tensions that occasionally marked earlier phases of the movement of population to the United States.

When the war ended in 1945, it was difficult to envision any substantial migration to the United States. The older period of free immigration had ended in 1925, and there seemed no prospect for a significant resumption of the movement. The quota legislation of twenty years earlier not only drastically reduced the total numbers who might enter, but also discriminated against the peoples of southern and eastern Europe, who were most likely in the near future to find immigration a solution to their problems.

The restrictive attitude remained basic to the permanent immigration policy of the United States. The plight of the refugees from Hitlerism in the 1930's did not call forth the slightest effort at amendment. Nor did the great war make an appreciable difference. Discussion of ameliorative efforts stopped at the point at which permanent immigration policy came into question.

Therefore, in 1945, when the dimensions of the postwar problem became apparent, all proposals for assistance to the displaced persons were phrased in terms that would not affect basic policy. Occasional expressions of dissatisfaction with the quotas, between 1945 and 1952, led to no specific proposals for change other than minor modifications to ease the rigidity of the system. The revision and codification of immigration law in 1952 (the McCarran-Walter Act) followed the old line of policy without significant deviation; indeed, it intensified the rigidities, discriminations, and injustices of the earlier legislation.

With the accepted official policy so rigid, aid for the refugees of Europe came largely through temporary measures that created exceptions to the general law. The United States had been active in UNRRA and in the IRO, and the President had early proposed that the statutes be amended to make room for a substantial number of victims of the war. However, it took several years of negotiation by the Executive Department and considerable pressure from public opinion before Congress was induced to pass the necessary legislation. The Displaced Persons Act of June, 1948, provided for the admission of approximately 400,000 newcomers of specified categories through the next four years. Extended and eased by subsequent amendments, this law made possible the only substantial contribution by the United States toward solution of this problem. At the expiration of the act renewed public pressure finally led to enactment in 1953 of another temporary measure that provided additional spaces for two more years, although under more restricted and more limited conditions. The last-named act never achieved even its shortsighted objectives. It came into effect while McCarthyism cast a shadow of suspicion over all newcomers, and narrow administrative rulings curtailed its effectiveness. In the spring of 1955 the resignation of Edward Corsi, appointed by the Secretary of State to expedite immigration under the law, dramatically illustrated the hopelessness of the conditions it set.

The only other step to relax the rigid restrictions of the permanent immigration legislation was a provision to permit members of the American armed forces to bring over, without cumbersome delay, spouses married abroad. Official policy was thus consistent: it regarded immigration as generally undesirable and tolerated exceptions only because of the pressing international problems of war and postwar relief.

Nonetheless, there are grounds for the belief that the official policy did not fully express the attitudes of the American people. The peculiarities of the domestic political situation in these years vested control over these matters in the hands of a group of legislators who represented only a minority of the population. An anachronistic committee system and factional divisions in the major parties put a cluster of rural and isolationist senators and congressmen into a strategic position from which they effectively frustrated the will of the majority. On such occasions as during the presidential election of 1952 when the issue was openly tested, public sentiment clearly favored a more liberal policy; only the means of implementing that sentiment politically have not yet been found.

The actual reception of the newcomers by the American people has reflected the favorable popular sentiment rather than the grudging official policy. The accommodation of the new arrivals in the postwar years showed a popular willingness in the United States to make places for the newcomers, in marked contrast to official policy.

Between July 1, 1945, and June 30, 1952, some 1,300,-000 persons came to the United States with the intention of settling permanently. This is a substantial number, although of course far smaller than those of the era of free movement before 1925. Of these some 760,000 were nonquota immigrants, that is, natives of the Western Hemisphere or individuals exempt from the quota laws by personal or professional status. Nearly 400,000 others were displaced persons admitted through the operations of the act of 1948. In addition 119,000 war "brides" joined their husbands and wives. The remainder were immigrants admitted under quotas through the normal operation of the permanent law.

Among the newcomers the largest contingents originated in the countries of older migration—Germany, England, and Ireland. There were also substantial contingents from Italy, Greece, Poland, and the Baltic lands. The annual migration from Canada averaged about 20,000 and that from Mexico and the West Indies about 8000.

All the relevant indexes show a favorable adjustment. Very few of the newcomers displayed by re-emigration a consciousness of their unwillingness or inability to make permanent homes in the United States. The number of alien departures fluctuated around 25,000 annually, a figure not greater than that of the 1930's. Most of those who departed were people who had entered the country before 1946, and the largest number were deported for some irregularity in their mode of entry.

The available information on adjustment within the United States confirms the impression of relative facility in adaptation. Data on settlement shows that the newcomers spread widely throughout the United States. The nonquota immigrants and the war brides had connections throughout the country, and the agencies responsible for assisting the displaced persons made an effort to distribute them everywhere. There was considerable concentration in the large metropolitan centers and some tendency among those who went to farms ultimately to drift toward the cities. But these trends were characteristic also of American population in general.

The economic adjustment now, as contrasted with earlier immigration, was eminently satisfactory. The new arrivals were drawn from the most vigorous age group; almost sixty per cent fell within the age group of fourteen to forty-five, as compared with forty-six per cent of the whole American population. Ready and eager to work, the newcomers were also more skilled than earlier immigrants: they numbered fewer operatives, domestics, and laborers and more farmers, craftsmen, proprietors, and professional people. They found jobs quickly and, furthermore, showed the capacity to capitalize on the opportunities they discovered in the United States. After a few years they showed the ability to move out of farm and domestic labor and into the more remunerative skilled employments.

The immigrants have encountered relatively few problems of social adjustment. They apply quickly for naturalization and fall in readily with the new way of life. Almost all have come in family units, a circumstance that has eased some of the shocks of transplantation. The rates of criminality, disease, and insanity seem lower than for the whole population. The refugees were unevenly divided among the three largest religious groups (forty-six per cent Catholic, thirty-four per cent Protestant, and nineteen per cent Jewish), but the distribution of all immigrants seems closer to the existing national pattern. All but a handful of the immigrants had some education and promptly learned English. Even in critical areas where housing has been short the newcomers have not been resented by the older residents. Indeed, the last decade has been remarkably free of xenophobia of every sort. Despite the tensions of the period and despite the fears aroused by the cold war these emotions have not been directed against the foreign-born. The hearings of 1952 evoked remarkably unanimous testimony on the success of their adjustment.

Several factors have been responsible. In the first place, the numbers involved have been relatively small. The average of annual admissions was less than 200,000. While this was sizable, particularly by contrast to the numbers in the two decades before 1945, it was minuscule by comparison with the earlier era, when the annual admissions were close to a million. Given the much larger population and the constantly declining percentage of the foreign-born, the problems involved were of a low order of magnitude. By their very fewness these newcomers were able to move imperceptibly into the streams of American life.

Furthermore, this immigration was strictly controlled and actively assisted. Federal and state agencies took a prominent part in recruitment and regulation and a large number of nongovernmental voluntary agencies were vigorously involved. The private agencies assumed responsibility for effecting the transition of the immigrants and aided them in every stage of adjustment. They supplied the newcomers with jobs and housing and with the material and cultural resources for rebuilding their lives in the United States.

These agencies expressed the interest in the newcomers of ethnic groups descended from earlier immigrants. The men and women who came off the ships in 1948 landed in a society in which they found waiting to assist them well-organized groups to which they were linked by sentimental, religious, or cultural ties. The newcomers found also functioning ethnic communities within which they could fall, going organizations and cultural media that could receive them and further the process of adaptation. Although there were occasional clashes of viewpoint and interest between the older and the newer comers, the way was open to successful adjustment.

The existing ethnic groups were conscious of their obligations toward the newcomers. They were also likely to insist that they had, by their own contributions to American life, earned a place in the United States for the new immigrants. Sensitive to the need of justifying their own position, the Italian, or Greek, or Polish, or Jewish Americans were determined to show that other Italians or Greeks or Poles or Jews were capable of becoming fully Americanized. While such groups as yet lacked the political power to recast the permanent immigration legislation, they were able significantly to further the success of the settlement of the new immigrants. In this process the growing emphasis on the rights of minorities and on the tolerance of differences was also helpful.

Finally, the America to which the immigrants came after 1948 had meaningfully changed since the war. In the process some of the old sources of tension had disappeared.

The economic change, for instance, had been drastic. In a period of booming prosperity the unemployment problems of the 1930's had disappeared, to be replaced by a perennial shortage of manpower. With no serious competition for jobs the addition of new hands was a boon; and the labor organizations no longer opposed, but favored, immigration.

By the same token the inflexible isolationism that had dominated American politics between the wars had all but vanished. Few now believed the United States could divorce its future from that of the rest of the world. Among the national responsibilities were the victims of the war in which the United States had been an active partner.

Whether they remained in the camps of Europe or became charges on the IRO, the United States would bear part of the cost of their support; and it was enlightened self-interest to aid them to self-sufficiency. In a large perspective also it was in the national interest of the United States to aid Europe to stability, and emigration was one of the means of doing so.

As the cold war became more intense, concern deepened, for the immigrants were now either its victims or drawn from among the potential allies in the struggle against totalitarianism. Such considerations altered the American attitude toward immigration despite the fact that legislation and official policy continued to express the views of an earlier decade.

Paradoxically, therefore, the most serious problems of adjustment were those of migrants who were not, properly speaking, immigrants, but American citizens. The Puerto Ricans who came to the mainland in the same period were uncontrolled and unassisted. They lacked established communities to receive them and suffered from some prejudice on account of their color. Their problems were far graver than those of the foreigners who came to settle in the United States at the same time. The experience of the immigrants, thus, was an encouraging omen of what might happen under a policy freed of the shackles of the national-origins quota.

CHAPTER XI

The Immigrants and the Diffusion of Ideologies

THAT SYSTEMS of ideas have power we know. They can move men to action and can influence the destinies of whole peoples. Yet the means by which they are communicated and spread are not often understood; and the question of means may, in this context, be critical.

Consideration of the problem of the diffusion of ideologies has been shaped largely by the point of view of the intellectuals who are most directly and most consciously concerned with it. The spread of ideas, from their perspective, is a process that operates through argument and conviction. Conceptions are examined and compared by logical men who choose among them. An idea thus moves through the conquest of opinion. This is the guiding premise of our efforts at propaganda and information.

It is well recognized, of course, that the process of conviction is not altogether rational; the past century has made abundantly clear the necessity for taking account of the nonrational aspects of human behavior. Nevertheless, discussion of the problem still rests largely on the assumption that ideologies are spread by some sort of debate, as a result of which men come to believe in the superior merit of one set of ideas over another.

This assumption conditions much of the current concern over the ideological aspects of the present world conflict. The necessity of a war for men's minds—the very phrase itself—reflects the notion that persuasion and the will to believe are the primary elements in the acceptance or rejection of an ideology.

Whatever its validity for the intellectuals, this assumption is certainly questionable when it comes to the broader strata of society which are the stakes of today's war of ideas. In the conflict now in progress the minds at issue are not simply, nor even primarily, the minds of the intellectuals, but those of men whose most deeply held beliefs are acquired not by argument and conviction, but by inherited tradition. It would be deceptive to think of the diffusion of ideologies among them as the product of the same process that animates the intellectuals.

The vast bodies of peasants throughout Europe and the Near and Far East who are only now being touched by the dominant strains of modern politics are an example. These people existed under ways of life fixed for generations, and integral with those ways of life were ideologies millennial in their firmness. It is shortsighted in the extreme to regard current alterations in their modes of thinking as if those were induced by any specific or immediate system of propaganda. If the ideologies of Russian or Indian peasants have shifted in the last half century, it was not through the impact of doctrines imparted through books or speeches, but through some deeper change in the structure of their societies. Marx in Russia or India is but vaguely the recognizable figure of the German nineteenth-century socialist.

The anthropologists whose work brought them into immediate contact with variant systems of beliefs have been most sensitive to the dimensions of the problem. Most often they have been disposed to regard ideologies as inextricably linked to the social and cultural milieu of the group involved, and therefore not subject to ready change. Some anthropologists, indeed, have accepted a kind of relativism on the basis of which every people's system of beliefs is deemed appropriate by the mere fact of its existence.

From this point of view alterations are almost impossible of achievement, and the diffusion of ideologies is a slow glacial process that can be only slightly affected by policy.

In general the anthropologists have been inclined to recommend that the social and cultural structure of a society, including its ideology, be accepted without direct efforts toward immediate alteration.

Such a course has obvious liabilities as far as policy is concerned. To put it most concretely and most bluntly, it surrenders the hope of transforming the basic value systems of the great masses of people who must be our allies in the near future. It involves the incalculable risk of materially strengthening groups whose ideas are fundamentally divergent from our own, and who would therefore in the future make unreliable partners. If it is not possible to spread the notions of democracy to men brought up in a patriarchal or traditional society, have we any assurance that the collaborators our aid now brings us will ever acquire an interest in our ultimate objectives?

Without in the least minimizing the real difficulties involved it may yet be that the problem is soluble. The American experience offers suggestive clues as to the nature of an operation in the present, for the essence of that experience was the spread of a complex of ideas to large groups of men initially hostile to it.

The American ideology, general to the nation despite the diversity of its people, is not simply a common heritage in the narrow sense; the bulk of Americans today do not have a common heritage. The antecedents of that ideology lie back in the eighteenth century, but the process by which it reached the mass of the population was slow, and extended through the nineteenth and early twentieth centuries. In the course of diffusion it encountered great resistance, with the outcome often uncertain. Comprehension of the factors that enabled it to take hold may throw light on some of the crises we must anticipate in the near future.

Let our point of approach be the 1830's in the United States. In that decade there could be said to be a well-defined American ideology, compounded from the doctrines of the eighteenth-century enlightenment, from the forms American religion took in its development from

Calvinism, and from the terms in which the descendants of Europeans explained their contact with the wilderness. The elements of that ideology were an implicit acceptance of the idea of progress and of man's perfectibility, a firm faith in the power of reason to transform the world, and the confidence that evil was a product of defective human institutions that could be rectified by human effort. The external expressions of this ideology took form in the years that followed and played a significant part in the life of the nation. On one level they included the certainty that the individual, by his striving, could assure himself of his proper goal, mundane success; on another they included the conviction that society could be reformed by organized movements to eliminate its imperfections. These ideas and the overt forms in which they were embodied were involved in all the crucial issues of the next hundred years.

In the century after 1830 some thirty-five million immigrants came to the United States. Among them were a handful of intellectuals who brought with them ideas close to those they discovered in the New World. But the great, the overwhelming, mass of newcomers were peasants displaced from the soil their families had inhabited for generations. They carried with them ideologies that had been firmly fixed for centuries and that were altogether different from those prevalent here. The peasants had no conception of the meaning of progress, reason was to them a feeble instrument, and evil was an omnipresent and conscious force of the universe. By contrast with the Americans these people were likely to be pessimists; their reliance was upon the power of faith and religion as a means to salvation, for they believed that the world in which they lived was not one that was capable of true reformation, much less perfection. Instead their earthly existence was only the prelude to a more significant life that began after death.

Yet the newcomers became a part of American society in the fullest sense; they did not remain sojourners, but lost their strangeness as a process of accommodation made familiar the ways of life and thought in their new home. Furthermore, they acquired the privileges of citizenship and before long were able to act as conscious and direct participants in the politics of the country.

The old Americans accepted democracy as a matter of course. Since man was essentially good and reasonable, he was capable of guiding his own actions in affairs of state as in other aspects of his life. As he cast his ballot he made the choices most in accord with his own interest and with the interests of the whole society. For the peasant, by contrast, reason was fallible and man imbued with evil, and democracy was therefore a rank delusion. Each individual occupied that status in life to which he had been called, and it made no more sense that a husbandman should vote on foreign policy than that a ruler should plow. More concretely, nothing in their experience in the Old World had prepared these people for the conception of citizenship they discovered in the United States; nor had they any inkling of the means by which they themselves would come to be the governors rather than the governed. Yet these peasants, as removed from political democracy as their counterparts in Egypt or India today, within a remarkably short time became habituated to the instruments and manners of popular control of government.

That happy outcome was not simply the product of persuasion or education. The immigrants did not accept the new ideas as a result of argument and debate; indeed, the effort to thrust strange conceptions upon them evoked only stubborn conservatism. This was a lesson painfully and invariably learned by the political reformers who occasionally accompanied the peasants in the migration to the United States.

The small groups of political malcontents from Ireland, Germany, Italy, Poland, and eastern Europe who drifted to the New World in the nineteenth century were members of the middle classes moved by political grievances against the undemocratic governments under which they lived. They had been far removed from the peasants at home and only approached them through the bonds of common language and common situation in the United States.

The émigrés conceived their role to be simply that of educating and leading a peasant following. They were, after all, educated, or at least literate, and capable of dealing with the native Americans on terms of relative equality. Furthermore, their ideas were already closer to those most prevalent here, and were expressed in the common nineteenth-century language of democracy, liberalism, and nationalism. The very motives for their emigration were such as to attract universal sympathy. Yet, in the decades of adjustment, the émigrés discovered they were not capable of supplying the mass leadership. Their most hopeful schemes came to nought in the face of the apathy or hostility of those they presumed to guide. They were no more capable of arguing the peasants over to their beliefs in the New World than in the Old.

Paradoxically, in fact, the political refugees remained less at home in the United States than other immigrants. The émigrés were often insensitive to the shadings of difference between their ideas and those they encountered in America. Their vision was limited by the ideals for which they had fought in Europe, and often those proved but slightly relevant to the problems of the New World. Their situation as a minority within a minority in the United States constrained them to attempt to exercise control by means which were sometimes undemocratic and often self-frustrating. In the end they were driven to a succession of intellectual and political compromises in the effort to hold their following. Only the very exceptional individual among them—such a man as Carl Schurz—was able to locate himself in a pattern of American ideas and values; and he did so by decisively fixing his sights on this side of the Atlantic. On the other hand, the great mass of immigrants, once they discovered they had access to power, learned to work toward a definition of their own interest and toward a perception of the ideological necessities of their situation.

The political involvement of the immigrants began at the comprehensible local level; while the issues of national policy still lacked meaning, those of the urban ward or rural county had a direct relevance to industrial laborers or subsistence farmers. These folk sought protection from the government against the hazards of the economic and social order, substitutes, as it were, for the traditional communal safeguards of the family and village that no longer existed in America. Their ideal was thus a policy of patronage.

Through much of the nineteenth century they found themselves in opposition to the dominant currents of American liberalism, in which laissez-faire elements were strong and which held to the ideal of a polity of regulation. The immigrants were therefore likely to find attractive the leadership of bosses and other political adventurers who could make meaningful promises to them.

The inadequacy of favors as the basis for political decision became increasingly evident, however, to the immigrants and, more so, to their children. After 1890 there was a search for more generalized concepts of political action to replace the free food basket of the ward boss. There followed a succession of experiments with labor and social legislation from which emerged the ideal of a polity of welfare, an ideal which could engage the interest and the loyalty of the immigrants and their children.

In the process American liberals discovered new dimensions to their conceptions of state action. By the 1930's such terms as "progressive" and "reform," which fifty years earlier had evoked no response from the immigrants, were now meaningful embodiments of their own hopes. And, although the connotations of the terms had changed enough to permit the kind of action these people desired, they rested still on an ideological base of optimism, progress, rationality, and reform. The change had meanwhile won the immigrants over to the basic ideology. Comparable developments in other aspects of American life illustrated the same kind of mediation.

Most critical in the pattern of adjustment was the attitude of the natives. Through most of the nineteenth century they approached the immigrants with confidence that any individual was capable of being an American and exercising the privileges of citizenship. At no point was there any serious disposition to limit political rights; indeed, in many states for a time citizenship was not even a prerequisite for voting. These practices reflected the assump-

tion that any man, whatever his background and previous
ideology, simply by exposure to American life became
American.

This belief was perhaps naïve. On occasion bitter conflicts followed disillusion when newcomers, given the
powers of citizens, acted not as other Americans, but in accord with their own divergent ideas. There were crises, for
instance, in the 1850's and in the 1890's that produced
short-lived nativist movements. In both cases the objective
was to limit the political power of the newcomers. Both
movements quickly collapsed. They failed partly because
they were contradictory to the very democratic ideology
they aimed to preserve. They failed also because the immigrants were accommodating themselves to American democracy and in other crises demonstrated their capacity for
dealing with the real problems of life in the United States.
Apart from these brief aberrations Americans clung to
their faith in the open quality of their Americanism, except
for the interval when racism clouded that faith.

Precisely that faith spread the American ideology
through the great mass of the immigrants. The fact that
they were treated as citizens capable of acting deliberately
in the affairs of the nation to which they had come was a
challenge to which the newcomers responded by so acting.
That created a situation in which the ideology they encountered, at first strange, became ever more meaningful,
not through argument, but through its appropriateness to
the way of life in which they were involved. Furthermore,
the fluidity of the ideology and of the society persuaded the
immigrants that their own hopes and needs could be encompassed within the existing order. Inherited ideas then
lost their relevance as the transplanted peasants absorbed
the new ideology through having lived it in practice.

It was critical, of course, that these peasants were transplanted, that they moved into the society the ideology of
which they absorbed. The problem is certainly different
and more difficult when it comes to spreading the same
ideology to peasants still fixed in their own society and still
surrounded by the institutions and forms that support a

divergent, indeed hostile, system of ideas. Yet it is possible to suggest a similar process of diffusion even under these conditions.

In the nineteenth century the same spirit that convinced Americans it was safe to leave their gates unguarded and to admit to the United States whoever chose to come there also drove them to an aggressive effort to spread their ideas to every corner of the world. The most important expression of this desire was the overseas missionary movement, which took form shortly after 1800 and by mid-century had carried bands of men and women to the remotest ends of the earth—to the jungles of India and Siam, along the coast of Africa, and deep down the rivers of South America.

The motives which sustained this movement were complex. But its impulses were truly popular, springing from some deep urgings of the American spirit. The movement drew its strength not from a handful of wealthy individuals, but from the contributions of thousands of relatively poor people. In the farmhouses of rural New England the housewives contributed each their mite to the salvation of the unknown souls in the outer darkness. They did so because it was an intimate concern of theirs that hundreds of millions of people remained unenlightened.

It is difficult now to assess the success of the missions. Yet there is considerable evidence of their genuine influence in many parts of the world. That influence was not the product of the particular theological doctrines the missionaries bore with them. It was, rather, the product of the diffusion of a way of life. The missionaries took with them more than tracts and Bibles; they carried with them also agricultural techniques, clothing, and the methods of modern medicine and hygiene. To the people among whom they came these were all inextricably bound together. As men learned to live the round of life the missionary practiced, they accepted also his ideology.

The weakness of the missions was a product of the inflexibility that limited their ability to adjust to the social and cultural needs of the peoples among whom they were planted. Yet they enjoyed enough openness of approach to exercise perceptible influence throughout the world.

There may be in these American experiences a clue to the general problem. The simple erection of steel mills and the building of railroads will no more bring democracy with them than will the export of slogans through the most skillful propaganda. Our ideas will have meaning and relevance throughout the world only as they explain a way of life. The diffusion of the ideology is thus bound in with diffusion of the way of life, in the fullest sense.

There are indications enough that men everywhere are prepared to accept both. If American movies are attractive, if *Reader's Digest* shows a remarkable penetrative power, even if Coca-Cola replaces the traditional wines, those are all signs of that readiness.

It is true that little in the background or antecedents of the peasant people has prepared them for either the way of life or the ideology. But just as men who have never seen the sea still recognize it at the first glimpse, so too those without a previous conception of democracy know it for the good it is at the first experience of it.

In that context the earlier adjustment of the millions of immigrants who were peasants, like those we seek now to influence, is instructive. For the immigrants also did not know in advance what they sought in the New World, other than a refuge from the Old, yet here they learned to recognize the worth of what they found.

Like them, the multitudes now who know only the unhappiness of their present situation may find in the new ideology and the new way of life a new "America" that will give them the dignity that is worth fighting for, and make of them the most valuable of allies.

CHAPTER XII

Israel and the Mission of America

FOR ALMOST a decade the Jews of the United States have had frequent occasion to examine the nature of their relationships with the state of Israel. Zionism had long since established ties of a sort with the settlements in Palestine. But the independence of Israel put into new and troubling forms the question as to the character of the loyalties that attach the Jew who is an American citizen to Israel, which is a foreign nation. Some long-standing precedents, some traditional historic attitudes may throw light on the whole problem.

The Jew is not the only American to encounter this question. In the years of trial through which we now live, all Americans have been compelled to give thought to the character of their connections with the people of the rest of the world. Few still believe that this country can maintain its own position in isolation from events in every remote corner of the earth. If our own role in world affairs is often uncomfortable and costly, it is yet one from which none of us can escape. In the future it will be even more important than in the past.

While this is a general obligation to which all Americans must be sensitive, the Jews of the United States are, in addition, subject to the necessity of making still another accommodation. They must consider also the nature of their specific relationship to the new state of Israel. In that consideration it will always be necessary to remember that this is a kind of relationship in which many other Americans are also involved.

This is not surprising. As a nation we were never detached from the rest of the world. Through much of American history the country grew by immigration. The descendants of more than thirty-five million immigrants now form a substantial part of our population. It was expected that the hundreds of thousands of newcomers should retain ties to the places of their birth. Until very recently it was usual that aid would flow back from the New World to the Old—in the form of remittances or as assistance in the face of unusual disaster.

Furthermore, the immigrants and their children continued to take an interest in the political affairs of the old country. One need only remember, in this connection, the struggle that lasted more than a century, on the part of the Irish Americans, to secure the independence of Ireland. As early as 1798 a group of Irish refugees fled, after the failure of the revolution that year, and organized here a liberation movement. Through the next half century the agitation continued. After the Civil War it actually produced an Irish republic in the United States which went so far as to mount an invasion against Britain's Canada.

Ultimately, of course, all that effort for Irish independence was successful. When home rule finally crowned the struggle, it was largely through Irish-American funds, men, and political pressure. Aftertones of that battle still linger among us in the fervent movement to assure the unification of the whole island.

In the same way the German Americans from the 1830's onward were preoccupied with the unification and with the ultimate welfare of their homeland. The Poles in the United States organized to secure the independence of the Republic of Poland while the land was still a Prussian and Russian province. Comparable developments will be found among Americans of such diverse origins as the Albanians, Italians, Magyars, and Czechs. Actually it did not even require the stimulus of a movement for independence to call such activities into being. Analogous movements appear among such groups as the English immigrants who had no concrete grievances of this order. These folk, too, maintained societies that attempted to preserve cultural attachments to Great Britain and to influence public policy on Great Britain's behalf. In a sense the desires of the Scottish-born Andrew Carnegie and the Irish-born E. L. Godkin to further Anglo-American unity were expressions of loyalty to the place of their birth.

The American Zionism of the last fifty years, therefore, falls into a well-established American pattern. It is not the eccentric behavior of a single group, but rather the normal outcome of the freedom of group life in a democracy.

It is only since the First World War that small—and unrepresentative—bodies of Americans have questioned the legitimacy of such actions. Significantly those who have been most violent in the outcry against hyphenates and divided loyalties are also those who have wavered most in their faith in the American democratic way of life.

Let us look for the moment not at the waverers, not at those small in faith, but at the articles of faith themselves. What was there about the Americans' conception of themselves that tolerated—indeed, encouraged—this multitude of activities?

We must recognize, to begin with, that these were not counted foreign activities. It was not simply Irish or Polish or Jewish immigrants who participated; all Americans had a stake in the same efforts, as individuals and through their government.

This involvement has sometimes been explained in crass political terms. When the Democratic President Truman recognized Israel, or when the Republican President Taft in 1911 abrogated the treaty with Russia as a protest against religious discrimination, some people attributed these actions to a bid for the vote of New York Jews.

Nothing could be further from the truth! For how, then, could we explain American intercession on behalf of the Jews of Damascus, as far back as 1840? The votes gained thereby were hardly consequential.

The record is consistent. Americans took a stand not merely on behalf of such people as the Irish, who were politically powerful, but also on behalf of the Magyars of 1848, who were not at all powerful. If the United States risked a break with Austria over Louis Kossuth, if men like Samuel Gridley Howe ventured their lives on behalf of Greek independence, it was not out of any petty calculation as to political advantage. Rather it was out of the conviction that some essential American interest was involved.

What was that American interest?

Before answering that critical question it will be worth our while to emphasize that its dimensions were wider than politics. The same interest led Americans to feel the obligation to relieve the sufferers of the Irish famine of 1848, or the Japanese earthquake of 1923. Awareness of that interest led thousands of Americans to contribute the pennies they could scarcely spare to support missionary activities in Hawaii, in China, in Siam, and in Africa. Somehow Americans believed it was a concern of theirs that in other parts of the world eight hundred million men lived in uncivilized darkness. That same concern to this day animates the Point Four program, leads American technicians and teachers to the stagnating villages of India, to the dank jungles of South America.

Why?

Behind all these activities lies the understanding that American interests do not end at the ocean's edge. On the contrary, this country is and always has been vitally concerned with the progressive diffusion of its democratic way of life throughout the world.

From the very start Americans assumed there was a universal significance to the New World experiment. On this continent, providentially empty, they were creating a society untrammeled by the outworn errors and the decadent institutions of the past. Here was the opportunity to realize to the fullest man's capacity for human dignity, for freedom and equality. It was the manifest destiny of the United States to create a model that would show the way to the people of the rest of the globe. It was *this* the revolutionaries of 1776 had in mind when they proclaimed, "The cause of America is the cause of mankind."

Therefore the struggle for Irish or Polish independence

was not simply an Irish or a Polish struggle; because freedom was involved, it was also an American struggle. And Irish Americans and Polish Americans participated fully in those battles, not as Irishmen or as Poles, but as Americans.

Nor was it un-American for a Yankee to expend his energies and funds bringing medicine and learning to Polynesians or Bushmen or Chinese coolies. In the deepest sense, in fact, this was service to the nation.

By the same token Zionism was regarded as the form through which an oppressed people struggled for liberation. Through the nineteenth century there had been widespread sympathy for the liabilities under which Jews suffered outside the United States, and Jews and other Americans had taken what steps they could toward ameliorating harsh conditions. Under these circumstances Zionism seemed to many one reasonable mode of relief. That Jews should labor to create a prosperous, progressive democratic state in Palestine comported perfectly with their interests as Americans.

In all these cases particular groups of Americans sustained and supported a country with which they had hereditary or traditional ties of some sort. *But they did so in terms of standards that had universal currency among all their fellow citizens*—the spread of democracy through the world, the self-determination of nations, international action for peace, the desirability of aiding small peoples against great oppressors. One did not have to be a Jew or an Irishman or an Italian to find justice in these arguments. The strength of ancestral attachments deepened the concern of immigrants, but this was a concern they could share with all Americans who had the same standards. Multiple loyalties were no problem; all Americans held them to some degree, for their conception of nationality was not totalitarian, did not dictate that they must love only the United States.

Americans have long recognized the right of expatriation, the extreme of divided loyalty. The only relevant questions are those as to the nature of the motives that lead to expatriation and their effects upon the welfare of the United

States. If an individual feels that his chances for self-fulfillment are greater outside the United States than in it, we shall be only the gainers by allowing him to seek his opportunities wherever he may find them. That was and is true in the cases of gifted artists like T. S. Eliot and Henry James. It was true of the great body of devoted missionaries of American birth who carried Western civilization and medicine to many parts of the world in the nineteenth century. It is true of American priests who go to Rome to enter the Vatican's service. It is true of those Irish Americans who may respond to Premier John Costello's appeal that they return to Erin to help rebuild it.

So, too, if there are among American Jews young men who find a challenge to their social imagination in the new life of the Israeli communal settlements, or a challenge to their constructive energies in the backward economy of the Near East, they will, in going, be following an American tradition of long standing. In their departure, so long as they think of halutziut as a pioneering movement dedicated to the furtherance of humanitarian ethics and democratic nationalism, they will only be spreading to another part of the world the ideals of American democracy.

For, through most of American history, the dominant conception of nationality has not been narrow, or restrictive, or exclusive, but, rather, broad and expansive. The attributes of Americanism were deemed appropriate to the people of the whole world. Just as any kind of man was welcome to come to the United States and to become an American, equal to any, so it was believed, the features of American life could spread everywhere. Any activity that assisted that diffusion was in the American interest.

This is still the conception dominant in our country. But it is not so readily applied now as it was fifty years ago. Under the tragic pressures of two world wars and of a society dizzily changing about them some Americans have found their confidence ebbing away. The disappointments of two unsuccessful crusades have deprived them of hope, have destroyed in some measure their ability to believe in the ideals for which those crusades had been waged. Insecurity and fear have possessed them, although their country's power is greater than ever before.

For such men nationalism narrowed down to a rigorous tribalism. It seemed safer to withdraw to the security of one's own kind, to find or create a pattern of homogeneity and uniformity, rather than to face the continuing risk of encounters with upsetting strangers. For the hundred-percenter, Americanism admitted no diversity, no partial or divided loyalty, no tolerance or difference.

In the atmosphere generated by this new and different nationalism some Americans began to resent the ties that held them to the world outside their borders, and were tempted to think all their difficulties had foreign roots. Hence the pathetic attempt, through isolation, in the 1920's and 1930's to escape the responsibility of diplomatic leadership. Hence the turn in immigration policy that brought an end to the long history of settlement and saddled us with the racist quota system. And hence the suspicion of every movement with international links. These are the sources of the demand for some exclusive loyalty, of the dislike of internal divisions or foreign connections.

Those who make these demands do not really speak for America; the appearance of support they attract is but a temporary product of the confusion and uncertainty of the times. As our true national interest emerges with increasing clarity, Americans have realized again that they are not an island cut off from the main, but that they are involved in the fate of a whole world; and they have responded through the United Nations, through Point Four, and through many other means to the obligations of their position. In the context of this broader, and more traditional, conception of the American national mission Jews and other Americans will continue to assist in the upbuilding of Israel.

A grave responsibility rests also upon the Zionists and other Jews engaged in the task. The forms of their aid and support must come in terms meaningful within the conception of American mission; they must rest upon the sense of justice and democratic hopefulness that animated comparable American activities in the past.

It is a mistake, for instance, to defend Israeli policy by a separate standard difficult to justify in general terms. A few American Zionists have thus been altogether too cavalier in their attitude toward the Arab refugees; a few were reckless in their apologetics for terrorism; a few have taken a hot-headed and unprincipled position on the UN decision to internationalize Jerusalem. These stands, even though by a minority, threaten to weaken the American Zionist case.

More important, it would be a grievous mistake to attempt to build up Israel by disparaging America. Officials who consider that American Jews are in exile, in time inevitably destined to be gathered together in Israel, are in error. Fund raisers who attempt to stimulate contributions by stirring up fears of future anti-Semitism here are also in error. The few Zionists who wish to stimulate emigration with the argument that a sound Jewish life is impossible in the United States are again in error. All these well-intentioned but mistaken people are ignorant of the true basis of American support for Israel.

The handful of extreme nationalists is only a small minority among the Jews, just as the hundred-percenters are only a small, if vocal, minority among Americans. Most Jews, in Israel and in America, realize that they will best serve both countries not by weakening, but by strengthening the confidence of Jews in their life in the United States.

In today's world, torn by the struggle between freedom and totalitarianism, democracy has no other future than that which the United States can preserve for it; and it would be hard to conceive the survival of Israel in any but a democratic world.

So long as Americans recall the importance of their role in spreading to the world the material and spiritual goods they have developed, there will be room enough for American Jews to maintain fruitfully the special ties history has given them with Israel. The best hope of a sound and creative relationship between Israel and the Jews of the United States, therefore, is that which rests upon faith in the traditional democratic mission of America.

CHAPTER XIII

The Returned Emigrants

As THE road turned and began to climb the hillside, we could look back down toward Olympia. There in the valley, where the fallen columns speckled with gray the green of the meadows, was the ancient site of the Hellenic games. It was hard to imagine in the solitude of this rolling countryside that here, for a thousand years, the Greeks had gathered from every end of the Mediterranean world to renew in sacred rites the ties that bound them in kinship and in devotion to the ancestral gods.

Jolting upward along the dirt road, which we shared only with an occasional peasant astride his leisurely donkey, it seemed appropriate that this should be our point of departure. The terrain grew more rugged, and soon we lost sight entirely of the smooth-flowing Alfios and of the whole universe of settled men. Only now and then the flocks grazing on the stony slopes gave a hint of human habitation—as they did more than two millenniums ago when Spartans fought Mantineans for mastery of the Peloponnesus.

Our destination was a mountain village. On the map we had located its name, Tropaia, dangling, as it were, in empty space a little north of the road we followed, a small place and inconsequential. This was the seat of the George Washington Greek-American Association. Here the emigrants who had once turned their backs upon their native soil had returned; like their remote ancestors, they had been drawn back to the place of their birth. Yet the proud letterhead of their association let us know that they had returned to their village not merely as Greeks, but as Americans also.

And we wondered whether we might not find in their experience some clue as to the nature of the loyalties involved in the shifts of masses of men by migration.

The currents of transatlantic migration had always flowed in both directions. The larger movement had been westward toward the New World's opportunities, but a lesser drift had also borne back to Europe those men who had tried American life and preferred the satisfactions of their former homes.

Already in the seventeenth and eighteenth centuries such occasional returned emigrants made themselves known in the records. After 1820, as the mass migration of western Europeans got under way, the temporary settlers became somewhat more numerous. But the difficulties of the journey still kept the total number low. Few men, having once survived the long weeks of privation in the steerage of the wooden sailing ships, would lightheartedly undertake a second passage, whatever the reason.

After 1870, however, steam diminished the terror of the Atlantic crossing. The time, the danger, and the cost of the passage all grew smaller. Ever more often, thereafter, the Europeans coming to the United States saw a way back still open after they landed. The number who left again, although always small in comparison with those who stayed, increased steadily.

Indeed, when the nineteenth century closed, there were among the newcomers at American ports some who arrived with no intention of staying. Young men, when times were hard at home, could come across for a few years' work, hoping by their labor to save enough to establish themselves back in the villages of their birth. These "birds of passage" left behind their families, lived alone, and set their sights firmly upon the return. Often such temporary migrations prolonged themselves indefinitely; and in time the young men grew old, were married and became the fathers of Americans, and lost the desire or hope of a second resettlement. But sometimes the older ties were strong enough to draw them back.

Of the sixteen million immigrants who came to the United States from Europe in the three decades after 1900 almost four million went back in the same years. In the easy times of a twenty-dollar ocean crossing some may well have drifted back and forth again and again, drawn to America by prosperity and high wages in some years, pushed back to their old homes by depression and unemployment in others.

The First World War and then the end of immigration reduced the volume of this transatlantic traffic. The cost of passage rose and men everywhere were more fixed in their places. But the hard times of the depression revived the movement. More than one hundred thousand left the United States in the harsh months of 1932 alone; and in the whole decade of the 1930's about a half million departed. Since then the tide has declined. Now some twelve thousand aliens and as many more American citizens annually return to European homes.

How many of these people now live in Europe is difficult to estimate. It seems likely that there are scattered across the length and breadth of the continent about three million Americans, that is, men of all conditions and degrees who have had some experience of life in the United States. In Poland and Norway, in Ireland, England, Italy, Greece, and Yugoslavia, these little islands of the twice-displaced radiate the influences of the New World into the surrounding society of the Old.

So much for history.

Only the history is not quite over. Even now the tourist draws to a stop before the gasoline pump in a remote village and is greeted by a voice rich in the intonations of Brooklyn or Chicago or South Milwaukee. As the car pulls away from the huddled cluster of little houses, the driver may wonder in passing how such familiar phrases come to be heard in such strange settings. What brought back the neat little elderly figure to sit for hours in the hard sunlight of the café terrace? After forty years in the fruit store on Halstead Street how do the aging legs find the pace proper to the rutted lanes of the older world? And what does the village make of these lost sons, as disruptive in their return as in their departure?

Those who have come back are a various lot—as different among themselves as those who once departed. Putting apart such well-known but unrepresentative figures as Lucky Luciano who moved through no choice of their own, the returned reflect in their condition and in their motives all the varieties of experience that might befall the immigrants.

Some are men who have never come to rest and are always in transit. On the bus riding into Athens from the airport we fell into conversation with the toolmaker from Lansing. We had seen him first standing bewildered in the monumental confusion of the customs shed and had noticed later his halting efforts to answer the inspector's questions in Greek. (When the TWA hostess interceded to translate, he reverted with relief and yet disappointment to English.) Now he stared eagerly through the window as the bus sped by the dark suburban streets, straining for a token of recognition. It was all strange to him.

No, he had never actually seen Athens before. When he had left his Macedonian birthplace more than forty years earlier, he had gone by way of Trieste, he thought, although he was not sure. (But it was a foreign place, he knew, and big, with many ships in the harbor.) Athens was strange, too, more like Lansing than he had expected; and he wondered what Salonika was like, where he would visit his sister. None of his family were left in the native village, for a glimpse of the image of which his eyes shifted ever and again vainly outward.

He was probably older than he looked; there were only a few flecks of gray in his hair. Still, he must have been no more than a lad in his teens when he set out for America, alone, to join friends. A good worker, he had not had too hard a time of it; and for some reason he had never married —which made it easier to get by. He knew Lansing well and had often been in Detroit. But he was the eternal lodger, nowhere really at home. And as we rolled into the lights of Constitution Square, he was the first to be out of his seat and stood impatiently at the door when it swung open.

It was not likely his quest would be successful. Already
by then, and again later, we had encountered many like
him. These men had never overcome the shock of emigration. They had stayed in the United States two years, or
twenty, or more, and, with greater or lesser facility, had
mastered the concrete details of American life. They earned
a living and stayed out of trouble, watched the movies and
paid taxes. But they could not regain what they had lost by
coming away—the sense of belonging, of participation in a
community. Passive in their attitudes, they were kept by
some numbing apathy from joining in the activities that
made other immigrants at home. Instead they looked backward and, in their longing, fancied they might fill, back
there, all the lacks of their empty lives.

Sometimes they put their dreams to the test of actuality
and retraced their steps. More often than not, they then
found the emptiness crossing back with them. The villages
had changed and they themselves had changed, and everywhere they seemed to carry with them their own particular
bleakness. As they leaned shyly at the bar, listening to the
other men's jocularity, it might be one world or another outside the curtained windows; it was all the same to them. If
they stayed on through inertia, or crossed back again, and
again, they never shook off the restlessness that disturbed
them.

It was worse if they had been failures even in the concrete details.

We determined to try lunch in the town's only restaurant. The hot afternoon sun poured into the dreary room
as we entered, emphasized the monotony of the line of
bare tables down its center. Bustling forward in a show of
enterprise, the proprietor led us to our places. I sat down
and the wobbly chair collapsed beneath me. The man
stood by in helpless indecision, his eyes shifting nervously
from the symbol of his futility on the floor to his indignant
wife glaring from behind the counter.

He, too, was an American, although the language now
came slowly to him. In Seattle he had been a long time in
the restaurant business. But it had not gone very well, and
in 1930 there had been hard times. So he thought he might

as well come back where a man could at least live off the soil. Only the bit of inherited land was not so good, and he was out of practice in the farming business. So he thought he would try a restaurant again. Times were not too good here, either, although he managed. Of course, he had a son over in the States who helped him out once in a while. He lingered as the woman set the plates before us; but his conversation ebbed away, and his thoughts wandered off to some inner concern of his own.

The official in Naples told us of a harder case still. Naturally the names were confidential. But there was this Italian who had lived a long time in a big city, say like Cleveland. He had worked hard and raised a family—three daughters and a son, all married now and with families of their own. After a while his wife had died and the old man got so that he could not hold a job any more; by then he was nearing seventy. It was a problem. The children were considerate, but they were none of them wealthy and they had to think of their own children. Besides, the old man would not be happy staying with any of them; he had his own ways and was always criticizing and just did not fit in. Anyone could understand that.

Then again there was all this talk about the old country. He was always telling them how nice it was, how kind the people were, how they always stuck together. When the idea first came to them, it seemed so simple they could not understand why it had not come sooner. Let the old man go back to live happily ever after with his sister who had kept up the family place. They would help out, of course, and would miss him. But surely he would be better off. At the jovial farewell before they drove him to the airport they made a little ceremony of handing him the ticket— one way.

Now he was a case. To the sister in Italy he had become a nuisance; he was not at all her picture of an American as he wandered aimlessly about watching other men at work and with hardly a lira in his pocket. She began to talk of the length of his "visit"; he was welcome in *her* home, of course; but soon, no doubt, he would begin to think of returning to *his* home. He himself was bewildered; little he saw matched his memories. He was no longer sure that he wanted to stay. But neither could he determine to go back to the children who had no room for him. Then, too, if he were to wish to return, there seemed no way of making them understand it. It had always been hard to talk meaningfully with them; now the ocean and the written page made it harder still.

At last there was a falling out with the sister, some petty quarrel that left him quivering with rage and resolved to leave. Penniless and with nowhere to go, he was at his wit's end when he turned to the consulate for advice. Months later when we left he was still a case.

Among the immigrants to America there were some who never managed to win control. They had left in the first place because home ceased to have room for them. They had not been able, in resettling, to fix roots firmly in the new soil. On either side of the ocean they were doomed to remain uprooted.

More numerous were men of quite another type, for whom the return was the culminating reward of their success in immigration.

We came out into the afternoon brilliance of Easter Sunday and remarked the two-toned Chevrolet with Virginia license plates parked before the hotel in Tripolis. When we drew to a stop at the little park on the outskirts of town, we saw the same car. The youth in the uniform of the Greek Army who sat idly at its wheel proved to be the nephew. His two American uncles had just come back for a visit, and with them his aunts and an American cousin his own age. We agreed that there was a notable family similarity between the two young men, stretching the truth a bit for politeness's sake. They were pleased to know that we, too, perceived the likeness.

We were almost friends by then. The Americans were eager to have us linger; they welcomed our presence as a momentary relief from the excessive intimacy of relationships long suspended and suddenly renewed. Perhaps also it was reassuring to speak English again and thus to establish a contact with home. On the other hand, they were anxious that we should think well of the country, of the town, and of their relatives. The park was not much; it could not come near, of course, what we had in the United States. But if we would come with them, they would show us something really worth seeing.

We strolled ahead with the elder of the uncles, a slender little man well into his sixties. His small-businessman's neat dark suit and sober tie with matching socks and handkerchief decisively set him apart from the motley holiday crowds we passed in the narrow streets. This, he repeated, would be worth seeing; they had planned their whole trip to be here on Easter Sunday. In fact, he confided to us, all those years in the States his most poignant memories were of this occasion. His brother and he had done well with the laundry—they had a big plant now with forty employees—but, to tell the truth, every time the month of April went by they really felt they were missing something.

At the head of the street we halted at the threshold of a small building. It seemed by its structure a garage, but this day it served another function. The gay crowd within overflowed into the street and we were at once made a part of it. We found ourselves sipping little glasses of resinated wine; and although the babble of many voices was incomprehensible, the laughter and good feeling were not. From the back there was singing, a kind of measured chant vaguely Oriental in its quality. We edged inward to see.

Over the floor were spread the glowing embers of a fire; and across it, dressed on sturdy wooden poles, were spitted four whole sheep. The animals revolved slowly among the thin wisps of smoke, turned lovingly by eager helpers on either side. We looked for the uncle who had guided us, but he was already lost in a circle of well-wishers. Jovial, without self-consciousness, he had dropped back into an experience deep in meaning for him. It was the goal of his coming back to be able to recapture a memory, if only once. For in doing so he gave a wholeness to his life, so that his satisfactions as a man were made one with his aspirations as a boy.

He was one of a numerous contingent. Regularly the ships at Piraeus and Naples, the planes at Ellinikon and

Ciampino deposit their throngs of nostalgic visitors. In families or in tours conducted by their fraternal societies they come back to enjoy the long-denied satisfactions that their American success now puts once more within reach.

The same longing for wholeness brings some emigrants permanently back to the place of their birth. In a small town on the way south from Florence hardly a fair day passes but finds a vigorous old man fishing dreamily by the lakeside. In his youth to sit thus was the prerogative of the gentry, and he had often thought how fine it would be to lounge there grandly without a care in the world. He had gone away and moved from place to place, become the maître d'hôtel of a well-known dining room in the United States and observed all manner of important people. All that while he still thought how fine it would be to take one's ease with a rod by the lake. And it was fine, now that his work was behind him and he had his competence, to make a placid familiar figure in the bright sunlight at the water's edge.

Such fortunate ones among the returned emigrants themselves put it simply. There are friends or relatives they wish once more to live with; they long to see again the cherished sights, to repeat again the precious acts of their earlier days. Or else, they explain, their dollars go a longer way in the old country. She had worked hard as a housekeeper for one family after another in New England, and now her little savings would buy her a nice property in County Cork. An income modest by the New World's measures goes a long way back here. Even a monthly Social Security check which in New York or Chicago would earn a man no more than a grudged corner in a son's apartment would here make him a person of consequence; the consulate in Athens alone disburses some five thousand Social Security and veterans' checks each month. Often the house of the American stands apart in its newness and neatness from the gray drabness of the rest of the village.

Through all the variations of these particular explanations runs a general theme. Those who were successful in the migration to America, who found the means of supporting themselves and established stable patterns of life in their new homes, could not, nevertheless, crowd out of their thoughts the memories of their old homes. For some among them, indeed, the ability to come back for a visit or to stay was a precious reward for their ability to make good in the United States. That is why those who return are more likely to seek out the villages of their birth than the impersonal cosmopolitan cities.

Sometimes, of course, the reward brings with it its own train of difficulties. A new loneliness assails those who have come back and who now think, with unexpected nostalgia, of the American places and persons they left behind.

In addition a host of nagging annoyances trouble them. "What a country," said the little man in the Piazza di Spagna. "I order coffee. Comes a little cup of tar. I want soap. Never heard of it. I buy some; they want to eat it. A bath? Sure! They take me outside, stand me over a hole in the ground, and pour water on me from a wine barrel. Some people!" The appearance of familiarity is repeatedly deceptive; a man comes with the assumption that he will fit back into a situation of fifty years ago, then finds the village has changed and he himself is no longer the same. Relatives known for years only at a distance prove at closer acquaintance deceitful or avaricious. Then again almost all who return nowadays are elderly and have imperceptibly become accustomed to American standards of comfort, sanitation, and medicine; they are distressed by the deficiencies of the old country. Occasionally advance calculations turn out to be overoptimistic; the cost of living is higher than expected for those who insist upon their usual brand of American cigarettes. A few returned emigrants worry about their citizenship; if they are less than sixty or did not live twenty-five years in the United States, they may lose their passports after three years' absence. Yet even these genuine problems rarely diminish the satisfactions of having returned.

The lingering attachment that draws back the emigrants, successful and failures, abruptly and permanently disturbs the villages to which they return. In widening circles the influence of the Americans ripples outward until it touches upon every aspect of the old way of life.

Part of that process we were able to observe in Tropaia.

When we left the main road, the grades of our climb became steeper and the terrain more rugged. At this altitude the warmth had dropped out of the air. Taking a succession of hairpin curves, we lost sight altogether of the valleys below. Then we crossed a ridge and saw spread across the mountain the scattered houses of the town.

In the square before the church the little group of loungers regarded us with suspicion. But we had no difficulty in locating the Americans. The small boy, sent scurrying off, was soon back, and following him, at a dignified pace, was the president, a sturdy man who bore his seventy years with power and confidence.

For a while we chatted idly and commented on the difficult road over which we had come. He smiled and pointed with his stick. It was over that same way that he had gone almost fifty years before, a youngster, really, although already married. There were many others like him who had nothing to do at home; and he had wandered over to Pyrgos, on the coast, in search of something with a future. He had not found that promise running errands for a local shopkeeper and before long he made the longer move to America. He had tried his hand at selling fruit and groceries in a number of Middle Western cities and finally settled down, a dealer of fish on Cape Cod. (Come to think of it, we in Cambridge had been practically his neighbors.) He had lived in the same town the largest part of his life and had done well, if he said so himself; someday, if we wished, we could see his name still carved over the entrance to the business block near the railroad station. But now he liked it back here in his own house. He had thirteen grandchildren in the States and flew across to visit them every few years. Still, he had the feeling he would like to spend most of the days left him here.

Of course, they had had terrible times in Tropaia. You could see the land was not much good, and the young people still had nothing to do. While the new hydroelectric plant was being built over on the Ladhon River, some of the men had found work and a cash income there. But the plant was now finished, sitting silent in the wilderness with only a few engineers to tend it. There was much talk of emigration, and some villagers had left for Australia and the United States. But the laws were not encouraging and this course promised no immediate relief to the economic problem.

Then, too, the war had opened a long period of disorder which was scarcely closed yet. The Germans and the Italians had never been able to control this mountain area. The guerrillas had taken over and had mostly run things after their own fashion. Only, once in a while, the invaders would come in and mete out savage retribution upon the guilty and innocent alike. One way or another those were not good years. And then after the war it had been hard to restore order. The communists were awfully strong in these hills and it was not easy to track them down. Even now, when they could not show their hand, they were still numerous and still dangerous, in a secret sort of way. The people were pitifully poor and they had not much faith in the government. What could you expect?

That was one of the reasons the Americans had started the association. It was curious, over in the States he kept being reminded he was a Greek; here he could not forget that he was an American. The village had many needs and the villagers were poor. More than that, it made him mad sometimes to see how folk accepted things as they were, how they listened to false ideas and were misled. It was necessary to do something.

The secretary had now joined us and took up the discussion. In a little village everyone has to help out, anyway. When a neighbor has trouble or the church needs a new window, nobody says anything; but they sort of look to the Americans. Who else has anything left over to spare? And usually they are not disappointed.

But then it seemed there ought to be more system to this. Right here, around Tropaia, in the district of Cortynia, there were almost fifty Americans, and they would see each other once in a while, elderly men all of them, from Beloit and Milwaukee and Canton, Ohio, and elsewhere. Then they thought it would be a good idea to form a society through which they could organize and work for improvements. They had in mind not only improvements that would make the towns more decent, but also such as would give the townspeople better ideas.

They were rather vague as to what they meant by the latter point. They had not mixed much in politics back in the States; and if you asked them about Republicans and Democrats, they only knew what they read in the papers. Anyway, most of them were American citizens and they had no desire to get into trouble with the government here. Still, there was surely no harm trying to straighten out the other villagers or to show them something about American methods. The old-timers who wanted everything to stay the way it was were against them, as were some of the younger hotheads who were maybe communists and suspicious of the United States. But the association was doing some good, the president hoped.

A boy of ten hurried by, balancing on his head a tray with the family dinner hot from the communal oven. "Look," the president said, "we are teaching them English." The lad stopped, ready to display his abilities, and the president beamed in pride.

Tropaia is not alone in feeling the effects of the returned. On the island of Khios a retired beauty shop operator of seventy comes back from Pittsburgh and feels the desire to do something; soon he has the school remodeled and a new road built. Elsewhere it is a church or a waterworks, a new mill or an olive press, or, as in Tripolis, a splendid modern hospital constructed out of the voluntary contributions of Greek Americans. The Americans, moved by the contrast between their homes on one side of the ocean and the other, are a continual irritant that will not let the village rest.

In the poor countries of Europe—and few countries on the Continent are not poor—their presence is of incalculable importance. In Greece one in three families is officially registered by the government as poverty-stricken. A succession of earthquakes while we were in the Peloponnesus showed how uncertain was this society's bulwark against disaster. Almost no one had the resources to survive unaided. It could scarcely be otherwise. After all, one eighth of the population is employed less than one hundred days a year and family incomes are correspondingly low. In Italy the percentage of poor may be somewhat lower, but not enough to reassure those who fear that the unrelieved burdens of misery may overwhelm the bewildered people with despair from which only the communists would profit. Everywhere the most bewildered and the most depressed are the peasants, the very group from which the bulk of the emigrants were once drawn.

The returned emigrants demonstrate that there is an alternative to the despair in which communism breeds. In that sense they are partners with the American Government in an effort that has already expended billions of dollars in Europe. But it is not simply the money they bring and the material changes they help effect that give importance to the role of the returned emigrants. For generations now departed relatives have been sending help back and the villages have grown accustomed to aid from overseas by remittances; the day we left the *Executor* carried four thousand aid parcels into Piraeus. Those who return continue such assistance in their own way; but they supply also the stimulus of another, more significant, kind of help.

Their own way of life is continuing proof that there is an alternative to despair. They repair the old cottage or build a new one which they fill with mechanical devices. They have a kind of nostalgia for the old customs, but when it comes to practical matters, they are altogether intolerant of tradition and are everlastingly suggesting new improvements. They are loyal to the old faith but impatient with popular beliefs, at which they sneer as superstitious. They seem ready to change the whole order of the universe with their ceaseless talk of how things are done in the United States. After all, who can deny the force of the argument from the experience of America?

There he stands, in his own person the most effective argument of all. He may be elderly now with long years of hard work behind him. But he wears the respectable suit, the white shirt and tie of the middle class, and he expects as his right a comfortable home. Yet he is no stray from the outer world of the gentry. He is not the flickering figure of a movie screen. He is a villager like themselves, whose family for generations labored beside their own, and who himself last left the square a miserable lad for whom there was no place at home. Who can persuade him there is no hope!

He will not even hear through the evasive complaint, "Well, in America it may be possible, but here . . ." He knows that there was no magic to migration. He calls to mind readily those who left with him but did not survive or for years eked out a precarious existence, scarcely less abject in the New World than in the Old. Now and then he can even point out, among those who have returned, a failure as helpless now as ever. America itself solved no problems; it only offered men the opportunity for creating solutions through their own striving for improvement. That, in the last analysis, is the doctrine he sets endlessly before his old compatriots—that change for the better is possible and attainable through their own efforts.

Put in concrete terms they can understand, the villagers often find the argument enticing. If only it were true! When we were invited to dinner in Tropaia, our driver, as was his custom, prepared unobtrusively to disappear. The president noticed and read him a lecture: "In America we do it differently. Why should you not be good enough to dine with us?"

Such questions, raised repeatedly, rock the ancient assumptions and habits of the village. The activities of the returned immigrants in their American Legion posts, in AHEPA, GAPA, and a host of other voluntary societies, show the men around them undreamed of means of social action. Even those who never saw the United States become members of branches of such American associations and begin themselves to explore the potentialities of democracy.

That is why the returned emigrant is often resented by those who resist change and prefer the settled order—by the gentry who profit from it, by the radicals resentful of any but the revolutionary change, and by the peasants bound to the *status quo* through inertia. To the gentry he is a nuisance who has moved out of his class without acquiring the values of their class. He may have wealth, they say, but no standards, and he remains a peasant without the peasant's virtue of submissiveness. To the communists and their allies he is the advance agent of Yankee imperialism covering over the corruptions of capitalism and impeding the cause of the revolution. Meanwhile the mass of peasants remain suspicious of his rise in station and not altogether certain that his wild schemes can be trusted.

Generally he is not himself aware of this opposition. In his eagerness to be liked, in his longing for identification with a community, he assumes all will think like him. It comes as a surprise to see sullen faces, to overhear snatches of malicious gossip. He can hardly conceive the mistrust aroused when he furthers what seem to him self-evident propositions.

That surprise is a product of his situation. He is a man not altogether like the other villagers, nor yet like the other Americans, but one who has lived in two worlds. He is not always capable of adjusting to the strains of that effort. But often enough he does succeed and thus draws together in his own experience and thinking the qualities of both worlds. That is his most useful role.

Every so often a letter from the provinces reaches the desk of an American official in the consulate or the information service of the United States in one of the European cities. The style varies and the degree of literacy. The letter contains local gossip or a report on politics or simply greetings. In any case, it represents a desire on the part of a returned emigrant to establish contact with his government.

The letter is routed around from one desk to another and comes to rest in the files. The officials themselves are sympathetic, particularly if they have been some time in the country and have actually come to know some of the people. But it is difficult to formulate a consistent policy with regard to those who come back, to treat them as either wholly American or wholly Greek, Italian, Irish, or Norwegian.

Back during the war the late Louis Adamic proposed a grandiose and romantic scheme for using the returned emigrants to transform Europe in the model of America. It was hopeless in its unreality, for the nations of the Old World have their own characters and problems, to which the experience of the New is not always directly relevant. The Americans who went back to Lithuania, Albania, and the other new nations of central Europe after 1918 had already painfully discovered that. Furthermore, any effort by the Government of the United States to use these people directly would not only be interference with the domestic concerns of other nations, but would also multiply the suspicions of their neighbors in the village.

Yet even without such effort the returned emigrants can be helpful, as they have been in Tropaia and as they were throughout Italy when the election of 1953 did much to save that country from communism.

Something can be done, moreover, to ease the uncertainties of their own situation. Earlier in the century, when the issues of American immigration policy were being heatedly debated, a bitter animus was often directed at the "birds of passage," as if they were somehow doing this country a disservice by going back with "our money." Traces of that prejudice still linger, as in the case of the citizenship provisions of the McCarran-Walter Act. The threat of loss of citizenship for those affected is an unmerited imputation upon their loyalty. It would be a small thing to relieve them of that fear and by this and any other possible means to let them know we understand the problems of their position and value their role.

Today, more than ever, we know that those who advance the interests of one part of the free world advance the interests of the whole. Indeed, it should be a comfort to know that scattered through many critical areas of Europe are hundreds of thousands of respected men whom migration imbued with an abiding affection for the United States. Each in his own way once made a contribution to America and now, returned to the land of his birth, still serves the country of his adoption.

"It's like a good son," said the president as we left Tropaia. "When he marries and comes to love his wife, he learns better to understand his love for his mother."

Notes and Acknowledgments

I. *The Origins of Negro Slavery*

The material in this chapter appeared first in the form of an article, written jointly with Mary F. Handlin, "Origins of the Southern Labor System," *William and Mary Quarterly*, April 1950. The complete documentation may be consulted there. See also Paul S. Taylor, "Plantation Laborer before the Civil War," *Agricultural History*, XXVIII (1954), and "Plantation Agriculture in the United States," *Land Economics*, XXX (1954), 141.

II. *One Blood or Many*

There is an extensive literature on this subject. For the period before the Civil War the most helpful secondary sources are: D. J. Boorstin, *Lost World of Thomas Jefferson* (New York, 1948); Charles S. Sydnor, *Development of Southern Sectionalism* (Baton Rouge, 1948); W. S. Jenkins, *Pro-Slavery Thought* (Chapel Hill, 1935); R. B. Flanders, *Plantation Slavery in Georgia* (Chapel Hill, 1933); B. B. Munford, *Virginia's Attitude toward Slavery and Secession* (New York, 1909); U. B. Phillips, *The Slave Labor Problem in the Charleston District* (Boston, 1907); and K. M. Stampp, "Fate of the Southern Anti-Slavery Movement," *Journal of Negro History*, XXVIII (1943), 17.

But the original tracts and argumentative works are more helpful still. The attitude of the Revolutionary generation may be gleaned from Thomas Jefferson, *Notes on the State of Virginia* (written 1781–1782. Philadelphia, 1801); and

St. George Tucker, *Blackstone's Commentaries* (Philadelphia, 1803), I, Pt. 2, Appendix, Note H.

The slavery controversy itself produced an abundance of defensive works, many of them conveniently compiled in E. N. Elliot, *Cotton Is King and Pro-Slavery Arguments* (Augusta, 1860). The shift of ideas can be strikingly traced in the debates in the Virginia constitutional convention, *Debates of the Virginia Convention of 1829–30.* See also: T. R. Dew, *Review of the Debates in the Virginia Legislature 1831–32* (Richmond, 1832); *Governor Hammond's Letters on Southern Slavery* (Silver Bluffs, S.C., 1845); S. H. Dickson, *Remarks on Certain Topics Connected with the General Subject of Slavery* (Charleston, 1844); J. K. Paulding, *Slavery in the United States* (New York, 1836); Thornton Stringfellow, *The Bible Argument: or, Slavery in the Light of Divine Revelation* (Richmond, 1856); Josiah Priest, *Slavery as It Relates to the Negro Race* (Albany, 1845); Wayne Gridley, *Slavery in the South* (Charleston, 1845); E. A. Andrews, *Slavery and the Domestic Slave-Trade* (Boston, 1836); and C. D. Meigs, *Lecture on Jerusalem* (Philadelphia, 1841).

Secondary accounts for the period after the Civil War include P. H. Buck, *Road to Reunion* (Boston, 1937); C. V. Woodward, *Origins of the New South* (Baton Rouge, 1951); L. B. Priest, *Uncle Sam's Stepchildren* (New Brunswick, 1942); Oscar Handlin, *Adventure in Freedom* (New York, 1954); and Oscar Handlin, *American People in the Twentieth Century* (Cambridge, 1954).

Among the more enlightening primary sources are: Helen Hunt Jackson, *Century of Dishonor* (New York, 1881), on the Indians; H. S. Fulkerson, *The Negro As He Was; As He Is; As He Will Be* (Vicksburg, 1887); E. B. Seabrook, *Ariel Refuted* (Charleston, 1867); and J. R. Hayes, *Negrophobia "On the Brain"* . . . *An Essay* . . . *upon the Negro Race* (Washington, 1869).

III. *Prejudice and Capitalist Exploitation*

The material in this chapter appeared first in "Prejudice and Capitalist Exploitation," *Commentary,* July 1948. The books criticized are: Carey McWilliams, *A Mask for Privilege* (Boston, 1948); Oliver C. Cox, *Caste, Class and Race* (New York, 1948); and A. Léon, *Conception Matérialiste de la question juive* (Amsterdam, 1946; translation Mexico City, 1950).

IV. *The Linnaean Web*

The materials for this chapter have been drawn largely from the writings of the men discussed in it. In addition to the works cited in the text the following have been the most revealing: James C. Prichard, *Researches into the Physical History of Mankind* (3rd ed., London, 1836); Charles Caldwell, *Thoughts on the Original Unity of the Human Race* (New York, 1830); S. A. Cartwright, *Slavery in the Light of Ethnology* (1852); Charles D. Meigs, *Memoir of Samuel George Morton, M.D.* (Philadelphia, 1851); Henry S. Patterson, M.D., *Memoir of the Life and Scientific Labors of Samuel George Morton, M.D.* (Philadelphia, 1854); Josiah C. Nott, *Collections on the Natural History of the Caucasian and Negro Races* (Mobile, 1844); Josiah C. Nott, *The Negro Race—Its Ethnology and History* (Mobile, 1866); [Joseph] Arthur, Comte de Gobineau, *Moral and Intellectual Diversity of Races . . . with an Analytic Introduction and Copious Historical Notes, by H. Hotz. To Which Is Added an Appendix Containing a Summary of the Latest Scientific Facts Bearing upon the Question of Unity or Plurality of Species*, by J. C. Nott (Philadelphia, 1856); Georges Pouchet, *Plurality of the Human Race* (translated, London, 1864); Charles Morris, *The Aryan Race, Its Origin and Achievements* (Chicago, 1888); Karl Pearson, *Grammar of Science* (London, 1892); C. C. Closson, "Dissociation by Displacement," *Quarterly Journal of Economics*, X (1896), 156 ff.; C. C. Closson, "Ethnic Stratification and Displacement," ibid., XI (1896), 92 ff.; Alfred H. Stone, *Studies in the American Race Problem* (New York, 1908); Charles E. Woodruff, *Expansion of Races* (New York, 1909); C. B. Davenport, "Geography of Man in Relation to Eugenics," in W. E. Castle et al., *Heredity and Eugenics* (Chicago, 1911).

The following secondary works have been particularly helpful: London Anthropological Society, *Memoirs, 1863–64*, I, 423; J. C. Greene, "Some Early Speculations on the Origin of Human Races," *American Anthropologist*, LVI (1954), 31; J. C. Greene, "The Discovery of the History of Nature; Natural History and World View in the Eighteenth Century" (Harvard University Dissertation, 1952); Edward Lurie, "Louis Agassiz and the Races of Man," *Isis*,

XLV (1954), 227; Ernst Cassirer, *The Myth of the State* (New Haven, 1946; on Gobineau); T. K. Penniman, *A Hundred Years of Anthropology* (London, 1935); Roy H. Pearce, *The Savages of America* (Baltimore, 1953); and William Irvine, *Apes, Angels, and Victorians* (New York, 1955).

V. *Old Immigrants and New*

The material in this chapter is drawn from a memorandum on the social characteristics of American immigrant groups, prepared for the President's Commission on Immigration and Naturalization, *Hearings* (Washington, 1952), 1189 ff. In addition to the references there cited, see, for the permeation of American science by racist ideas, the reviews of Madison Grant by F. A. Woods, *Science*, XLVIII (October 25, 1918), 419; and Ellsworth Huntington and Leon S. Whitney, *The Builders of America* (New York, 1927).

For the general background of the immigration restriction movement see John Higham, *Strangers in the Land* (New Brunswick, 1955); and Barbara M. Solomon, *Ancestors and Immigrants* (Cambridge, 1956).

VI. *The Horror*

With a few fragmentary exceptions the materials for the history of American family life have been quite untouched by historians. The problems treated in this chapter have rarely attracted the attention of scholars. For suggestive insights one must, rather, turn to such novels as E. M. Forster's *A Passage to India* or Joseph Conrad's *Heart of Darkness*.

Yet the data for the study of these problems is abundant and, used with care, extremely rewarding. The writings of Horatio R. Storer, of Boston, are representative of the thinking of orthodox medical men. These include: "Cases of Nymphomania," *American Journal of the Medical Sciences*, October 1856; "Is Abortion Ever a Crime?" *North-American Medico-Chirurgical Review*, January, March 1859; "Studies of Abortion," *Boston Medical and Surgical Journal*, LXVIII (1863), 63; *Why Not? A Book for Every Woman* (Boston, 1868); *Is It I? A Book for Every Man* (Boston, 1867); "On the Decrease of the Rate of Increase in Population Now Obtaining in Europe and

America," *American Journal of Science and Arts*, XLIII (1867), 141; (with F. F. Heard) *Criminal Abortion: Its Nature, Its Evidence, and Its Law* (Boston, 1868). It is significant that the views of such conventional physicians as Storer on these questions largely coincided with those of the immensely popular lecturer and writer on phrenology Orson Squire Fowler. Among the widely diffused writings of the latter are: *Love and Parentage, Applied to the Improvement of Offspring: Including Important Directions and Suggestions to Lovers and the Married Concerning the Strongest Ties and the Most Momentous Relations of Life* (published, 1844; 40th ed., New York, 1855); *Amativeness or Evils and Remedies of Excessive and Perverted Sexuality. Including Warning and Advice to the Married and Single* (published, 1844; 40th ed., New York, 1855); *Sexuality Restored, and Warning and Advice to Use Against Perverted Amativeness, Including Its Prevention and Remedies* (Boston, 1870); *Private Lectures on Perfect Men, Women and Children, in Happy Families; Including Gender, Love, Mating, Married Life, and Reproduction, or Paternity, Maternity, Infancy and Puberty; Together with Male Vigor and Female Health Restored, and Their Ailments Self-Cured, &c., As Taught by Phrenology and Natural Science* (published 1878; New York, 1880).

Writings by other authors of various degrees of respectability include: Charles Knowlton, *Fruits of Philosophy. An Essay on the Population Question*; A. M. Mauriceau, *Married Woman's Private Medical Companion* (New York, 1847); John Ware, *Hints to Young Men, on the True Relations of the Sexes* (lectures, 1847–1848; published 1850; numerous editions to, Boston, 1879); William A. Alcott, *The Physiology of Marriage* (1855; 25,000, Boston, 1860; also published "By an Old Physician," Boston, 1856); Dr. Charles S. Woodruff, *Legalized Prostitution: or, Marriage as It Is, and Marriage as It Should Be* (Boston, 1862); Elizabeth O. G. Willard, *Sexology as a Philosophy of Life* (Chicago, 1867); Mortimer A. Warren, *Almost Fourteen, a Book Designed to be Used by Parents in the Training of Their Sons and Daughters, for Present Modesty and Nobility, and for Future Fatherhood and Motherhood* (New York, 1897); National Christian League for the Promotion of Purity, *Constitution and By-Laws*, 1910–11. The reference to the Mormons is from an article by Dr. Charles H.

Furley, "Physiology of Mormonism," *Boston Medical and Surgical Journal*, LXVIII (1863), 507.

The influence of these factors runs through the literature on slavery in a subtle but, nevertheless, explicit fashion. In this connection see among the works cited in the notes to Chapters I, II, and IV particularly those of E. B. Seabrook, H. S. Fulkerson, Wayne Gridley, J. K. Paulding, S. H. Dickson, Governor Hammond, Georges Pouchet, and C. C. Closson.

The only secondary account to have dipped into this material is the unpublished dissertation at Harvard University, N. E. Himes, "The Practice of Contraception and Its Relation to Some Phases of Population Theory" (1932). There are some perceptive comments, in another context, in Hannah Arendt, *Origins of Totalitarianism* (New York, 1951), and in Kurt H. Wolff, "On Germany and Ourselves," *Southwest Review*, XLI (1956). See also Arthur Mann, "Gompers and the Irony of Racism," *Antioch Review*, XIII (1953), 103.

VII. *American Minorities Today*

For illustrations of the racist thinking in the decade of the First World War see the note to Chapter V above and the following representative works: William B. Munro, *The Invisible Government* (New York, 1928), 41–42; Irving Babbitt, *Democracy and Leadership* (Boston, 1924), 210; H. L. Mencken, *Men v. The Man* (New York, 1910), 110; Ralph A. Cram, *Nemesis of Mediocrity* (Boston, 1918), 40; Paul Popenoe and Roswell Hill Johnson, *Applied Eugenics* (New York, 1918); William McDougall, *Is America Safe for Democracy?* (New York, 1921); Carl C. Brigham, *A Study of American Intelligence* (Princeton, 1923). For the development of the Negro in this period see particularly Gunnar Myrdal, *An American Dilemma* (New York, 1944); and C. Vann Woodward, *The Strange Career of Jim Crow* (New York, 1955). Data on lynchings may be found in the *Negro Yearbook*. For other ethnic groups see Oscar Handlin, *American People in the Twentieth Century* (Cambridge, 1954); and Oscar Handlin, *Adventure in Freedom* (New York, 1954). For the development of desegregation in the two years after 1954 see New York *Times*, March 18, 1956, IV, 9. For immigration problems see Edward Corsi, "My Ninety Days in Washington," *The Reporter*, May 5, 1955.

VIII. *What Happened to Race?*

Most of the material in this chapter was originally part of the memorandum for the President's Commission, cited above, Chapter V. On the development of genetics see L. C. Dunn, ed., *Genetics in the Twentieth Century* (New York, 1951). For a review of the psychological literature see Paul Kecskemeti, "The Psychological Theory of Prejudice," *Commentary*, October 1954. See also Oscar Handlin, ed., *The Positive Contribution by Immigrants* (Paris, 1955).

IX. *The Larger Significance*

For additional material bearing upon these problems see Oscar Handlin, "Group Life within the American Pattern," *Commentary*, November 1949; Oscar Handlin, "Freedom or Authority in Group Life," ibid., December, 1952; and Oscar Handlin, *American People in the Twentieth Century* (Cambridge, 1954).

X. *The Newest Immigrants*

The material in this chapter was originally prepared for the World Population Congress, Rome, September 1954. See also: United States Displaced Persons Commission, *Reports* (semi-annual, 7 vols., 1949–1952), and *Final Report* (1952); President's Commission on Immigration and Naturalization, *Hearings* (82 Congress, 2 Session, 1952), and *Whom We Shall Welcome* (1953); *Statistical Abstract of the United States*, 1953; United States Immigration and Naturalization Service, *Reporter* (monthly, 1946–1952); and Jacques Vernant, *Refugee in the Post-War World* (1953).

XI. *The Immigrants and the Diffusion of Ideologies*

This essay appeared first in *Confluence*, September 1953.

XII. *Israel and the Mission of America*

This essay appeared, in another form, as "America Recognizes Diverse Loyalties," *Commentary*, March 1950.

XIII. *The Returned Emigrants*

This essay appeared originally in the *Atlantic Monthly,*
July 1956.

In the preparation of this volume and of the materials
that have gone into it, I have been indebted to the stimulating interest and assistance of Edward Weeks, Elliot E.
Cohen, and Nathan Glazer. In every stage of writing I have
depended upon the devoted collaboration of Mary F.
Handlin, who has shared fully the burdens of research and
composition. The incomparable resources of the Harvard
College Library have been invaluable to our work. I am
also grateful to Cecily Tourtellot, who prepared the manuscript with efficiency and dispatch.